The Adventure of Affirming

Reflections on Healing and Ministry

The Adventure of Affirming

Reflections on Healing and Ministry

Anna Polcino, M.D.

Affirmation Books
House of Affirmation
Whitinsville, Massachusetts

Published with ecclesiastical permission

First Edition
© 1986 by House of Affirmation, Inc.

Library of Congress Cataloging in Publication Data

Polcino, Anna
    The adventure of affirming.

Includes biographical references.
    1. Spiritual healing. 2. Christian life—Catholic authors.
3. Women—Religious life. 4. Pastoral medicine—Catholic
Church. I. Title.
BT732.5.P55 1986   248.4′8209   86-8005
ISBN 0-89571-030-7

Cover design by Patricia Mullaly, Circle Graphics.

Printed by
Mercantile Printing Company, Worcester, Massachusetts
United States of America

Dedication

In gratitude to my patients in Pakistan, Bangladesh, and the United States, and to the residents of the House of Affirmation.

For it is they who have taught me how to live, how to suffer, how to die, and in dying enter into eternal life.

Acknowledgments

Chapter Two, "Ministry to the chronically ill," was originally published in the October 1982 issue of *Hospital Progress* as "The Chronically Ill, Handicapped, Aged: Guidelines for Effective Ministry" and is reprinted with permission.

Chapter Three, "Belonging—longing to be," first appeared in *Belonging*, E. J. Franasiak, editor (Affirmation Books, Whitinsville, Mass.: 1979).

Chapter Four, "From Loneliness to holiness," was originally published in *Loneliness*, James P. Madden, editor (Affirmation Books, Whitinsville, Mass.: 1977).

Part of Chapter Seven, "Psychotheological community," first appeared in the September 1975 issue of *The Priest* and is reprinted with permission.

The other chapters were originally talks given to various ministerial and medical groups.

Every attempt has been made to credit sources. If any sources have not been acknowledged, please notify Editor, Affirmation Books, 109 Woodland St., Natick, MA 01760 so that credit can be given in future editions of this book.

Reflection by a former resident of the House of Affirmation

In the beginning was the Word
and the Word was with God
and the Word was God.
Proclaimed by four
as a light overcoming darkness
But the Truth
of my exile from tender love
barred all beginning from the Word
And in the darkness hovered
my child's heart
The intense yearning for light
yielded trust
yielded surrender enough
for the journey.
Another,
in truth a mother,
celebrated my Epiphany
So that
at the very center
I heard
"Talitha Kum."
The child
now knows blessing
knows for all eternity the love
That shall enable her
to hear the Word
to receive the Spirit
To know the Light
that no darkness shall overcome.

Eileen

CONTENTS

Foreword

The primary source of meaning in life is affirmation. True affirmation is far more than speaking a word of encouragement or giving a compliment. It focuses on the very being of the other person, on that person's goodness as a unique human being. It presupposes openness, confident expectation, and consistent attention to all that happens in others, to all that they are not able to express, and to all the potential good within them, even though they do not yet suspect that future good.[1]

Affirmation is the essence and core of all mutual love. The most tender, delicate, indeed healing touch is that I encourage the other person to be who he or she is, immaturity and shortcomings included. I do so not out of fear, but out of free choice. Affirmation is precisely what is needed for achieving appreciation of self and authentic identity in relation to others and the created order. John Paul II reminds us:

> It is exactly in this that the fundamental ethical trait of love is expressed: it is an affirmation of a person—without this affirmation, love does not exist. Permeated with a proper attitude concerning the value of a person—and such an attitude we termed affirmation—love reaches its fullness; it becomes what it ought to be: an integral love. Without this affirmation of the value of a person, love disintegrates and, in fact, does not exist at all, even if the reactions or experiences coming into play are of a "loving" (erotic) character.[2]

In all his actions and parables Jesus teaches us that the union of human persons creates an atmosphere for growth and healing. Jesus Christ whose Body is the Church offers us, too, the gift of being affirmed members in love; in his Body we know a new dignity. The Church, rich in its tradition, ever fresh in its articulation, offers strength, nobility of being, and an opportunity for

11

growth, healing, and health. Our Christian understanding of the Mystical Body hits at the very essence of what the *scientiae humanae* seemingly are just discovering.

The idea of affirmation opens new perspectives not only for individuals but for society as a whole. It is evident from what has been written over the past twenty-five years that much more new and bold thinking is required if we are to meet the challenges of the future. *The Adventure of Affirming* by Sister Anna Polcino invites us to reflect on the psychology and theology of affirmation. From her vast experience as a missionary surgeon in Pakistan and Bangladesh, her role as the foundress of several therapeutic House of Affirmation communities in this country and abroad, and her influence as a past instructor in psychiatry at the University of Massachusetts Medical School, she brings together a series of essays, reflections upon healing in ministry, which she has not only taught but lived. A woman of religion, a woman of medicine, and a woman of affirmation, Sister-Doctor Anna Polcino encourages our faith and challenges our thought.

Thomas A. Kane, Ph.D., D.P.S.
Priest, Diocese of Worcester
Publisher, Affirmation Books
Natick, Massachusetts

April 21, 1986
Feast of St. Anselm

Endnotes
1. See Thomas A. Kane, *The Healing Touch of Affirmation* (Whitinsville, Mass.: Affirmation Books, 1976).
2. John Paul II, quoted in Andrew N. Woznicki, *A Christian Humanism: Karol Wojtyla's Existential Personalism* (New Britain, Conn.; Mariel Publications, 1980), p. 38.

Introduction

Although our society claims to be enlightened about emotional problems, we still find that it often does not allow those who minister to others to be weak and vulnerable. With the changes in the Church since Vatican II, some understanding is beginning to grow that priests and women and men religious are real human beings. However, there are still many people who treat an emotional problem as if it were a spiritual problem. "Where's your faith? . . . If you just prayed a little harder, everything would be fine." But for a devoutly religious person, faithful in prayer yet struggling with depression or anger or interpersonal problems, such comments are painful.

We all need healing within ourselves. Life is full of pain and struggle. Sometimes we have serious doubts about our faith; we may be plagued by physical illness. Or we are overwhelmed with an emotional problem. But doubts, sickness, and problems can be a time of spiritual growth and development. At such times we need to accept where we are. We can use our struggles, our doubts, our illnesses to grow closer to God.

I have seen this in my own life. For nine years, I was a missionary surgeon in Pakistan and Bangladesh. Women in those cultures could not see a male doctor. I was the only woman surgeon in Pakistan, so I was very busy. But standing for long hours in surgery and enduring the effects of the climate led to a serious case of arthritis and brought me back to the United States. I was forced to reevaluate my calling. How could I continue to serve God if arthritis crippled me? I had always wanted to study psychiatry and my illness gave me the opportunity. Even confined to a wheelchair, I could still practice psychiatry.

In 1970 during the early years of my psychiatry studies, Father Thomas Kane and I were asked to begin a counseling center for sisters in the Worcester diocese. The sisters had found that when they went to counselors who did not understand religious life, they were told that their emotional problems were vocational problems and everything would be fine if they left religious life. Many of them were dealing with painful emotions in the wake of the changes brought by Vatican II, and needed counselors who respected religious life. Soon priests were also coming for counseling.

By 1973, we saw a need for a residential center and the dream of a psychotheological community was born in Whitinsville, Massachusetts. Most therapeutic communities have a psychoanalytical base. But we decided that the center would address not only psychological needs, but also spiritual needs. We would use a combination of psychology and theology to help the people who came to us.

We use the word affirmation because everyone needs affirmation: to be accepted as they really are, just because of their being, not for what they do. To grow into a complete person, we need someone outside ourselves to help us. Without the love and acceptance of another person, our own self-esteem cannot grow. We cannot initially affirm ourselves.

Some religious professionals do not have people who can affirm them. The community at the House of Affirmation allows people to be affirmed by others. For some, their stay at the House of Affirmation is their first experience of real community—love, intimacy, trust. Later on, they can affirm themselves by remembering.

As I have continued on this journey of affirmation, the healings of Jesus in the gospels have come back to me again and again. Jesus cared not only for the person's physical needs, not only for the person's emotional needs, not only for the person's spiritual needs. He treated men and women as whole people, created in the image of God to love and to serve others. The miracle of Christian service is that as we care for others, we are healed as well. When we accept a vision of health, which includes physical, psychological, and spiritual wholeness, we are on the way to true holiness.

Sr. Anna Polcino, M.D.

I.

The Challenge to Affirm

Chapter One

Called to be healers

*N*ow more than ever, the Church, the people of God, need the unique witness of each of us. It matters not what task we perform, be it cook, teacher, plumber, nurse, administrator, clown, psychotherapist, physician, parish minister, lawyer, or spiritual director. Love and not just expertise is needed and we all have the capacity to be lovers. It is not what we do, but what we reveal to the world that matters.

Our leadership position is based on the fact that God has called us to do his work and has given us whatever we need to respond effectively. God has invited us to join in a style of personhood which is life-affirming and life-creating. We are called to be artisans and authors of a new humanism. The Church is the healing community and we are all healers.

Let me suggest a definition of healing: "Healing is a satisfactory response to a crisis, made by a group of people, both individually and corporately."[1] There are a number of advantages to using this definition. It does not mention any medical words, so the contribution of parish ministers, social workers, physicians, psychiatrists, parents, brothers, sisters, neighbors, and others can all play a part in the response to a crisis. The definition includes not only the doctor and patient, but covers all those men, women, and children involved in the crisis, even those whose part is limited to refusing to concern themselves.

This definition also makes possible a single theology for both a ministry of healing and a ministry to the dying by recognizing a purpose and profit in both types of crises.

While it is true that we have Christ as a model of resignation to God's will, we also have the example of his active healing of the sick and afflicted. Christ's resignation was not a passive attitude but one of affirmation, a choice to accept. Therefore, while we accept the suffering God sends, we do so in an active spirit, doing what we can to improve our health, and not passively resigning ourselves.

Another important aspect of this definition is the idea of a group or team united in the healing work, rather than isolated skilled professionals acting without involvement. The model can be a family working through the physical or mental handicap of a child or the terminal illness of a member without depending on an institutional routine. It still allows for the help of healing specialists, such as doctors, health professionals, clergy, and others who can encourage or advise the group.[2]

The definition leaves open the processes used by those who do the work. Everything—penicillin, prayer, psychotherapy, sacrament, surgery—is allowed, and the quality of work is measured by its fruits, not the factors used. Remember, every crisis is an opportunity, psychological and theological, for both the individual and the group. If it is grasped positively, it results in a new balance at a higher level. Every crisis is a psychological and theological opportunity to react creatively and to reach new levels of maturity.

To call another to life—this is one of the most basic tasks of healers. It is also to call one's self to life. It means to help one another discover the real meaning of life so that each person may become the unique individual God intended. At a time when so many people feel unaccepted and alienated from self, family, community, and society, it becomes a ministry of healing that calls forth again the consistent factors of reverence and compassion that have always historically defined the art of medicine.

The healer, in a sense, is a person of authority, one who enables, develops, and prepares the possibility for realizing the potential of the persons entrusted to his or her care. It is necessary that we take the lead in this healing ministry in the modern world.

Our witness is to develop a healthy sensitivity, a reverence and compassion for individuals along with an awareness of the assets and liabilities inherent in any human being. If people are to be made whole and not merely cured, there must be an increased awareness of the need for an integration of their physical, mental, social, and spiritual development. All activities, whether on the individual, social, political, national, or international level, are interrelated. They all strive for humankind's liberation, which is the freedom from all bonds that prevent us from developing into the mature and free persons that we are meant to be, by God's design.

Our mission as healers is to believe in people and call forth the wholeness potential in each of them. This belief is rooted in and demonstrated through living the gospel values. We have the capacity for effective healing by establishing mutually favorable relationships through intimacy, nurturance, intuition, understanding, and tenderness.

As healers we must be in touch with our own thoughts and feelings and be willing to share them with others, accepting ourselves for who we are and acting openly on such awareness. Being for others is closely linked to the ability to be for self. Therefore, we as healers should realize that we are in the process of becoming, and actively pursue opportunities for our own growth.

In order to be healers, we must be in an ongoing process of relationship to God. We manifest this through both personal and communal prayer. As this relationship develops, we are more in touch with ourselves and spontaneously seek the growth of others. Prayer is the force integrating our being and our relationship to others.

We must be open to the unknown and effectively manage the ambiguity of the present. Creativity and flexibility must be a way of life for us.

The source of greatest satisfaction for us as healers is the growth of others. We must give our energy, time, and talents to bring this about. We should appreciate change, growth, and health in others when they occur, and be diligent and patient in the facilitating process.

We need to be supportive of our community, whatever it might be. As a sharing member of our community we find it to be an integral part of our becoming.

As healers we are concerned about the continuity and longevity of our ministry. We envision the future, risk in the present to make it possible, and actively support the insights of others to create that future.

In summary, we as healers are stretching persons who plan the healing of others, who purposefully choose ways in which we can best be of service to others, ourselves, and God. We are concerned with affirming life and healing and wholeness.

In healing ministries we share ourselves. We are the presence of Christ to others; we choose life for ourselves and others and thus witness to the healing ministry of the Church.

Endnotes

1. R. A. Lambourne quoted in John Turner, *The Healing Church,* (Belfast, Ireland: Christian Journals, 1978), p. 66.
2. Thomas A. Kane, *The Healing Touch of Affirmation* (Whitinsville, Mass.: Affirmation Books, 1976), pp. 30, 31.

Chapter Two

Ministering to the chronically ill

*E*very community contains chronically ill persons, whether they are in a hospital, a long term care (LTC) facility, a halfway home for the mentally ill, or a home where family members are physically or mentally handicapped or just elderly. Pastoral caregivers have many opportunities to serve these persons and their families.

The Church's attitude toward the sick is one of care and concern. It seeks to strengthen and support the sick in, for example, the rites for the visiting and anointing of the sick. In eucharistic liturgy the Church also shows its realization that the sick are a very special part of the congregation, even though they may be physically absent. They participate intensely in the saving death and resurrection of Christ; they participate in the mystical body.

A major problem the pastoral care minister faces, however, is the way cultural surroundings influence the chronically ill. Chronically ill people are bombarded by advertisements telling them how to avoid pain and weakness and enjoy better health. The message—implicit or explicit—is that being sick is to be avoided or prevented. People who are already sick want to be cured because they feel they are in an undesirable and bad condition. They think that because they are ill, there is no value in their present condition and no chance of happiness. They do not fit into the lives of those who are healthy. Illness is a shame, and being ill is out of place. If they are sick, they must conceal it and pretend they are perfectly healthy, or else they must hide themselves away in an institution, separating themselves from the healthy so that they will not disturb others' way of life.

For those who have a short-term illness, or who suffer the results of an accident, sickness is also a difficult time; however, they can look forward to joining the ranks of the so-called healthy again. The chronically ill have no such hope. Therefore the minister must become aware of this unconscious attitude society has toward illness and find a way to help them incorporate illness into their lives. One possibility is to think of *healthy* as meaning sound, solid, and whole. To be healthy is to be whole and to have integrity in one's physical, psychological, and spiritual dimensions. This attitude makes of life a unified harmonious whole and gives a place to illness, allowing it to contribute its significance to the meaning of life.

This definition of health as wholeness can make a difference in the ministers' attitudes toward the sick. They can help the sick man or woman to see that happiness is possible in this challenge to live more deeply. There is no cause for impatience or resentment. Being ill can, as a paradox, lead to new depths of happiness. This attitude, in turn, gives value to what the sick person is experiencing and suggests that this individual has something vital to offer to and share with others. If society develops this understanding of health as wholeness, people will appreciate, respect, and share with the ill person and his or her family.

Attitudes toward chronically ill, handicapped

Spirituality for the chronically ill is a wide-ranging subject. The ill may be young or old; they may be in an institution or cared for at home. The variety of handicaps to which they are subject makes each person unique.

Those who develop a chronic illness after years of good health may feel resentful. Their pain destroys their belief that they are in control of their lives. They have to battle with despair, fear, and depression. Not only do their physical lives change, but their relationships with family members and close friends change. There may be increased tension in the family as new roles are created. The chronically ill person may experience deep loneliness as old friends suddenly seem too busy to visit. Those who minister to the chronically ill must be conscious of these factors.

Those who experience a handicap also face new challenges. They must battle with daily frustration and constant struggle over their limitations. They may have to contend with lower self-esteem and the prejudice of others. They endure awkward stares and rude comments. Even worse, sometimes they are ignored by a healthy person or they are viewed as mentally inferior because of their physical handicap. Those who minister must not focus on the handicap but view the person in an integrated way.

Special problems of the mentally ill

Despite people's relative sophistication about illness, this same attitude of discomfort is sometimes evident toward those who are or have been mentally ill. Some mental disorders have physical causes: a brain injury or a disease that affects the nervous system. Many, however, arise as a desperate effort to cope with crises, failures, or inadequacies—all the results of anxiety and stress present in life. There are degrees of normality and mental illness, and both can be present in a person at once. Healthy persons develop habits, attitudes, and actions that enable them to live with a certain amount of comfort in their situations and without too much anxiety or stress. If some attitudes or actions are not appropriate or cause increasing anxiety or stress, these persons' behaviors will reflect one of the patterns of mental illness.

Actually, some situations should cause extreme stress and tension, and it may be possible that some people considered "well adjusted" are actually unaware of their situation's full dimensions. One example would be the person who does not show any emotion at a loved one's death. Mental illness may mean, for the person who suffers it, a call to a deeper health, to an integrity that takes fully into account the dark side of reality. It can be the "dark night of the soul," mentioned by both St. John of the Cross and St. Teresa of Avila. I think this expression refers to what are often daily experiences of ordinary lives—the losses, successes, pains, and aches.

One source of anxiety that can lead to mental illness is a sense of being unacceptable or unlovable, of feeling inadequate as a person. This anxiety can produce an unrealistic effort to be perfect and pleasing to everyone, combined with a hesitancy and lack of assertiveness that come from being unsure of others' affirmation. If this becomes a neurosis, it will seriously interfere with the person's ability to function. This behavior has several consequences. Although these men and women want to deserve affirmation and love by being so good that no one can find fault with them, their efforts to be perfect and their transparent plea for affirmation will more likely drive people away. The other sad aspect of this situation is their deep inner knowledge that no one is perfect; they find it difficult to believe in any proffered love. This attitude may lead them to test others' love by being a problem to them.

Aging parallels chronic illness

Another group that is deservedly receiving increasing notice is the aging. Older persons who are perfectly healthy may discover that their experience parallels that of the chronically ill, although aging is a normal process. Their powers are increasingly limited; the activities that once filled their days have become remote, as have the people with whom these activities were shared. The aging may find themselves more and more alone. Those who lived their working days looking forward to retirement when they would have enough money or time to do what they wanted find themselves with physical and often financial limitations, the victims of subtle prejudice, stereotyped as deteriorating mentally and physically. The elderly may find their self-confidence slipping as they recognize a slowing of their powers and experience a fear that aging might bring senility. The most difficult fact for them to face is that the decline is not temporary, but eventually leads to death.

Spirituality and holistic concepts

What constitutes effective ministry for these men and women and their families? Because of the holistic concept of health, the minister should first be interested in all aspects of a person's health—physical and psychological as well as spiritual. There may be pragmatic matters that would help the family, such as getting in touch with social agencies or volunteer organizations. People often do not know what is available to them. Really listening to the ill person may give hints on what can be done on the concrete level, for instance, obtaining food stamps. Those who visit the chronically ill should look at their surroundings. What is lacking? Missionaries have known for centuries that preevangelization is often necessary. As one missionary said, "People cannot listen to you talk about God when their stomach is empty." The foundress of the Society of Catholic Medical Missionaries, Mother-Doctor Anna Dengel, was very aware of this. In the missions, members work for the physical and psychological well-being of the people before preaching Christ to them. Therefore, before speaking of God to the chronically ill, one may have to take care of their physical needs.

An important principle to remember is that men and women can be whole and healthy spiritually, no matter what their illness or handicap. Therefore, one must help them to spiritual well-being. Spirituality is not one dimension among many in life; rather, it permeates and gives meaning to all of life. The expression itself indicates wholeness in contrast to fragmentation and isolation and human beings' dependence on God, the source of life.

Spiritual well-being affirms life with all its negative circumstances, not despite them. It is not optimism which denies or overlooks life's realities; it is the acknowledgement of life's destiny. In the light of that destiny, it is the love of one's own life and the lives of others and the concern for one's community, society, and the whole of creation. A person's affirmation of life is rooted in participating in a community of faith. In such a community, one grows to accept the past, to be aware and alive in the present, and to live in hope of fulfillment. This attitude is especially important for those with a physical or mental handicap or any illness.

Growing toward wholeness

All people are called to respond to God in love and obedience. As God's children, people grow toward wholeness as individuals and are led to affirm kinship with others in the community of faith as well as the entire human family. People affirm life in the context of their relationship with God, self, community, and environment. They see God as the creator of life who first affirmed them, as the source and power that wills well-being. Under God and as members of the community of faith, people are responsible for relating the resources of the environment to the well-being of humanity.

Another important principle is that people never fully attain human wholeness. All through life it is a possibility in process of becoming. In the Judaeo-Christian tradition, life derives its significance through its relationship with God. This relationship awakens and nourishes the process of growth toward wholeness in self, crowns moments of life with meaning, and extols the person's spiritual fulfillment and unity.

This principle is especially important for those who serve as pastoral ministers. The idea that the term *normal* has a wide range and that none of us is completely whole is an important fact to share with the chronically ill. The minister must first establish a relationship with the patient. Sometimes the man or woman has never learned to trust. Any unresolved conflicts that have been experienced through the years may become more prominent. It is important to allot sufficient time to build up trust. Too many deadlines will limit effectiveness. Time, which includes willingness to listen patiently, is one of the most important gifts to share with the chronically ill.

The minister must also cultivate an attitude of listening. Often, nothing specific can be done to help the ill person; one can only listen as he or she expresses feelings. In the process, perhaps the ill one will say something that will enable discovery of the healing power within. One of the current concepts in health care is that each individual has the innate ability to strive for wholeness.

In short, it is important to help the patient and the family to find meaning in the situation in which they find themselves. Look for possibilities to help all concerned to live satisfying, meaningful lives.

The attitude of sympathetic listening

The five stages Elisabeth Kübler-Ross, M.D., has listed in the process of dying—denial and isolation, anger, bargaining, depression, and acceptance or affirmation—are also experienced by the chronically ill. In listening to these persons, the pastoral minister tries to understand their basic attitude, find where they are in the process of becoming, and work with them to improve their life. Some people already have a deep faith. The minister's task, then, is to share that faith, to help deepen it, and to provide continued courage.

Realizing the particular problems the chronically ill face helps in sympathetic listening for what may not be actually expressed. Pain and how human beings endure it are a mystery. Some people can hold a conversation while enduring intense pain; others with lesser pain are reduced to suffering inaction. The patient's attitude has a great deal to do with how much pain he or she can bear. Anxiety and anger over the sickness compound pain, whereas affirmation raises one's capacity to endure. Persons who do not expect to get better, who have abandoned hope of recovery, are less able to withstand pain. Those who feel isolated from family and friends or from significant human companionship have more difficulty coping with pain than those who have been able to preserve their previous relationships.

Isolation and boredom can grow as an illness continues for a long time. Patients gradually lose contact with their previous active life, and their world closes in around them. Sometimes pain makes even reading impossible. During this time, sickness gradually weans a person away from roles, achievements, and most immediate interpersonal involvements. Such a process is painful, but it can open the way to a greater appreciation of simple things. For example, the weather, the perceptions of the senses, and the memories of particular joys in life become more important. Gradually, the ill can come to rest in their humanity and find serenity in existence itself.

A long illness can call a man or woman to a profound spiritual growth, to a genuinely humble self-acceptance, to accepting and embracing God's will (even when it conflicts with personal desires), and to a purified sense of human meaning in relation to God. The lived experience of illness has many depths, and each one brings a particular challenge and the possibility of profound significance. No two people have the same experiences, however, and no one set of directions can guide ministers in their encounters with the chronically ill. They must experience each patient's illness and help each one to discover God's call to a deeper dimension of life. This is empathy.

Principles guide effective ministry

Effective ministers to the chronically ill are guided by several general principles. They must examine their own inner lives and question their own wholeness. They must define their attitude toward the physically or mentally handicapped, the elderly, and those with long-term illnesses. Western culture and the attitudes of society are bound to influence ministers' attitudes; awareness of this influence is essential.

Even the minister's attitude toward ministry itself needs examination. No one can do everything alone; anyone who tries to do so will burn out quickly. Instead, caregivers should unite with others—priests, religious, and laity—and mobilize resources to aid in ministering to the chronically ill and their families. Sometimes medical professionals, although competent, are not healing persons. On the other hand, a caring relative or neighbor can provide a strong healing presence. Anyone can become a healing person by helping the patient and the family to communicate fully, seek and give information, and share feelings. Being sensitive to the chronically ill is important, and admitting one's own vulnerability reassures the patient.

Those who deal with the chronically ill are called to face, and perhaps adjust, their own attitude toward death. Some physicians and nurses see death as a failure, and many people have fears about it. Feelings and beliefs about death affect life and feelings and actions. It is essential to face these feelings honestly. Those ministering to the ill must also realize that they did not learn everything they need to know in college, seminary, novitiate, or theology classes. A basic knowledge of human psychological growth and fundamental skills in and knowledge of the principles of counseling are useful. The development of team ministry—clergy working with women and men religious and laypeople—deserves consideration. When dealing with the elderly, young people can be very effective. They can brighten the days of the aged while learning from them.

Giving and receiving essential in ministry

Practical guidelines enhance the pastoral minister's work with the chronically ill, the handicapped, and the elderly. Some of the following may be helpful.

1. For home visitations, call before visiting; set arrival and departure times. Sense when not to visit, and as a rule, make visits short. Be alert for signs of fatigue or pain.

2. Sit down. Get at eye level, touch, and establish real contact. Listen. Even a short visit will have more meaning.

3. Send something regularly: a note, a card, a prayer, bits of humor or odd information clipped from a newspaper. Anticipation is important. But remember that a visit, when appropriate, is the best gift.

4. Be authentic. Avoid false cheeriness or empty words. Saying, "You look great," to a person suffering in body or spirit is brushing aside pain. A hug or a pat on the arm may be all that is needed.

5. Offer specific help to the patient or family: babysitting, an errand, transportation.

6. Avoid criticizing the patient's care. Such comments can be detrimental and add anxiety.

7. Let the patient be the guide in his or her needs and wants instead of imposing your own ideas. Ask, "What would you like me to do for you?" Be available.

8. Let the patient give something, however small or intangible.

9. See the patient as a person, not as an illness or a handicap.

10. Let a dying patient find the release of entering into all his or her feelings and unfinished business. Those close to the patient can help in the letting go of life.

Where compassionate people are gathered together, there is concern for one another as individuals. As one becomes more of a healing person in ministry to the ill, there will be less need to ask what to say, what to do, and how to cope. Ministers will pray for God to work through them and will move from the position of observer to enter into the other's experience, sharing it in some way. They will grow more compassionate and more aware of the way all living beings are interrelated. With their help people can learn to accept each other as they are and realize that their calling is to make the best of what they are, not to live up to abstract ideals of health.

Illness is a collision with human limitations, a harsh and uncompromising reminder of the reality of finiteness. It forces the sick to come to terms with the reality of the human condition and, through them, confronts society with a sign of contradiction, a challenge to truth. Society wants to forget that all living things must suffer and die, while illness reminds it that life does indeed include suffering and death. This process of growth through pain and suffering goes on throughout life; no valid basis exists for a complacent sense of *having arrived.*

Illness can lead sufferers through the pattern of letting go of dreams, emptying themselves, and placing themselves in God's hands in a way that echoes Christ's own death and resurrection. The critical challenge of nearly every type of chronic illness is an affirmation. It is more than resignation, which can be a sullen surrender to inevitable defeat, and more than abandonment, which no longer hopes for anything. Affirmation hopes for meaning and value in illness, not necessarily for a cure. By acceptance or affirmation, illness is embraced as the present reality, and the ill person finds assurance through Christ's suffering that what he or she is doing is worthwhile.

Those who minister to the ill find that the ill, in turn, minister to them. Each learns from the other, is inspired by the other, and, as the ill show Christ's suffering, the healthy concerned find that they are calling one another to life in the spirit in a truly Christian way.

Chapter Three

Belonging—longing to be

*T*he word "belonging" evokes one of two feelings in us, depending on our background. Some of us feel sad, even melancholy, because we have experienced so little love or affirmation in our lives or because we are struggling to discern where to belong or to whom to belong. For us, belonging is rather a longing whereby we feel lonely, deserted, rejected. Perhaps what was once present to us is now absent. Perhaps we have been near and now find ourselves far from God. Others of us, when we hear the word "belonging" feel joy, for we have been blessed with much. We belong to persons, to groups, to the Church. We have friends and a solid conviction that we are part of the lives of others.

I perceive belonging as a longing to be, longing to be a friend, longing to have a friend. Today many religious and clergy feel the need for a friend in a way that they have never felt before. The reasons for this need are many. All of us are affected by the world in which we live. Since Vatican II, many structures of religious life have disappeared, taking with them a certain security. In the past few years, the so-called sexual revolution has changed society's opinion of what is morally acceptable. We have been asked to get in touch with our feelings and to express our emotions openly. As a result, the apostolic demands on religious and clergy have increased, requiring heightened emotional involvement and consequent emotional pain. The workers among us are fewer; as many of our companions have left religious or priestly life, we have lost friends. Because the pace of our lives is faster, our personal involvement is more complex. The religious community we entered has undergone changes; so we are living in a way we could never have foreseen. In addition, the excitement that we experienced in the early days of dedication to our ministry, which perhaps compensated for our lack of deep relationships, is no longer with us. The daily drain of our demanding apostolic situations brings to the surface deeply felt emotional needs that we may never have experienced before. Eventually, the time comes when the tasks in themselves are not fulfilling, and we look to personal friendships for fulfillment. This need for friendship is part of everyone's life. We all hunger to be more than we are, to go out of ourselves to others. Such a hunger can be fulfilled only by love, by the opportunity to touch the life of another, to love and then free that person, leaving that individual better as a result of my having known him or her. Many persons who long to have a friend experience problems because they do not know how to be a friend.

Christ gave us an example of friendship: "As the Father has loved me, so I have loved you. . . . I shall not call you servants any more. . . . I call you friends. You are my friends if you do what I command you" (John 15:9-15). We know that Christ loved John in a special way, that he wept over the death of his friend Lazarus, and that he loved Mary dearly.

Self-acceptance and fear

Friendship implies intimacy. Religious and clergy need to realize that they must accept themselves in order to have a meaningful relationship with another, even God. This acceptance depends upon our concept of self. We must reaffirm ourselves as human beings who are sexually alive. This reaffirmation is a lifelong process. Some religious and clergy are afraid of friendship. Although they have developed physically and intellectually, they are stunted emotionally because they have repressed their emotions. The ability to experience a deeply personal relationship with another develops only through emotional growth. Such growth is based on self-love, the basic form of love, which makes all other loves, including friendship, possible. Only by loving ourselves can we grow to love others and the Lord.

Friendship is important for religious and clergy today. It is always good to have a friend. We have to abandon the unhealthy ways we were taught to act in the past and learn to cultivate friends. We must love others without possessing or exploiting them. We must let others come close and know us as we are while we strive to know them as they are. In so doing, we can achieve an emotional bonding or union with other men and women. We know and like each other as we are, not needing genital involvement.

Certain fears can act as psychological blocks to friendship. These fears include: (1) fear of sexuality, including fear of sexual "contamination," and sexual inadequacy; (2) fear of anger and increased irritability (As two people reveal themselves more intimately to each other, they will find that they are not perfect. Thus we must deal with anger in close relationships.); (3) fear of dependent relationships (Many of us cannot permit ourselves to need, to show weakness. Thus much promiscuity is a struggle of one person to dominate another.); (4) fear of intense feelings of personal inadequacy, which can make us hide our true selves and wear masks or play roles in interpersonal contact; and (5) the fear of being vulnerable or hurt, when the intimacy of real friendship demands that we permit ourselves to be weak and vulnerable. Some of these psychological blocks may require professional help, but solitary reflection that gives us insight into and an understanding of ourselves helps, and is often enough.

Intentional friendship, not coupling

Coupling is the model in society today. Our first experience of it occurs as we view the coupling of our parents. In coupling, there is a giving over and a taking, an entry into another and a leaving of self. In coupling, each person both experiences a new freedom through a common unity and abandons a certain freedom through a sexual oneness. Two spirits, two bodies, two emotions become one. Each surrenders to the other and compromises to preserve the oneness. The two must exclude others because there are dimensions that cannot be shared.

Coupling cannot be the model for religious and clergy. For us, the model must be intentional friendship, whereby the two establish an open bonding, relinquishing possession. Together they share no dimension that they cannot share with another. The friendship is always open to others; it is not exclusive, but rather inclusive. Complementarity is the dynamic of this unity. Because the two celibates have sacrificed the freedom to establish their oneness in flesh, they are free to enjoy each other as the separate persons they are. Their fidelity to each other rests entirely on trust. There is no ownership. The two may crave physical bonding, but they do not need it.

Religious and clergy who are the model for this type of friendship do not ask how far they can go, for they recognize their commitment. Friendship cannot be legislated. A strong embrace will lead to other acts only between some persons. The quality of the individual commitment determines the course of the friendship. Intentional friends appreciate the uniqueness of each other; they do not need to make the changes that would result in oneness. As they remain the two together, they cannot soothe each other physically as couples do, but they can trust each other and remain faithful to that trust.

The spirit of celibate friendship

Models for celibate friendship between men and women can be found in Church history: Clare and Francis of Assisi, Teresa of Avila and John of the Cross, Jane Frances de Chantal and Francis de Sales. These saints were able to realize great things for the glory of God at least partially because of their friendships. In the earlier days of the Church, such friendships were praised and considered very much in keeping with the Christian spirit. Today we must recapture that spirit of celibate friendship.

A friendship is not something for which we shop. A gift from God, it comes quietly and slowly. Like all gifts from the Lord, it is not for the two friends alone; it should nourish the total lives and apostolates of both. Through the friendship, God is asking for more dedication and more commitment to him and to his people. The two friends treat each other with respect, and they support each other. They help each other to become more honest, more open, more transparent before God. The goals of their lives, not their desire to remain geographically close to each other, are the determining factors in their choice of apostolate and in their openness to mission.

Although we can long for friendship, we cannot create a friendship. But we can create an atmosphere conducive to receiving this gift when it comes. In Church history, one can also find unhealthy friendships. We must be aware of such pitfalls and be honest with ourselves, for we cannot live double lives.

Johann Rake has described friendship as

> . . . an encounter between two or more persons in a mutual sharing of space and time, embodied in a given culture, involving interaction and communion in light of some interest in one another and in shared truth or shared search for truth, resulting in an enduring nonexclusive relation which is lived as a gift of affinity, affection and personal history, and occasioning the autonomous growth of the person involved.[1]

Accepting our sexual and emotional natures

We Americans are considered friendly people, but while we may be good at casual relationships, we are not necessarily good at forming deep friendships. Sometimes we cannot form such relationships because we do not recognize and accept our emotions. We may instead deny them or reject them. But to avoid pain is to miss an opportunity to grow. We religious and clergy often grow intellectually but not emotionally. Our education and formation provided us with knowledge we could impart. We acquired skills so we could share the truths we were learning about God, human beings, and the world in which we live. But today, instead of being asked to serve people by supplying them with truth or answers to the problems they face, we are being asked to communicate with them personally and individually. We are being asked to listen to their needs, to share their struggles, to allow them to know our deepest attitudes, values, faith experiences, struggles, and weaknesses.

This challenge brings with it problems that arise from the sexual and emotional natures that God has given us. Our sexuality is an integral part of our lives. Every one of our interior and exterior activities has a sexual aspect. It is impossible for human beings to be asexual in anything they do, including communicating with God. All of us in the Church owe it to God, as our Creator, and to ourselves to accept the maleness or femaleness God has given us. We must recognize the sexual aspect of all that goes on within us, especially within the context of our interpersonal relationships. In our culture, when people use the term "sexuality" they usually mean "genitality." Genitality actually refers to the arousal or use of the genital parts of the human body. We religious and clergy have made a free choice not to use the genital aspects of our nature. But we cannot as a result give up our sexuality.

One of the difficulties of living the celibate life is the spontaneous and indeliberate arousal of genital feelings and desires. We religious and clergy know that our relationships with certain persons whom we find humanly appealing tend to produce at times more or less strong genital reactions within us. Moments of such feelings are inescapable in the context of the apostolic, shared, deeply transparent lives we experience in intimate contact with men and women and God. While we must struggle to achieve impulse control, we may experience such feelings as tenderness or as the warmth of a heart filled with gratitude, friendship, or love. These feelings are partly psychological and partly physical. They are also closely related to our thoughts and our imaginations, which elicit affective responses. These responses include our feelings, emotions, passions, and moods. (Feelings are mild emotions; passions are very intense ones. Moods are the emotional states in which we remain for a certain period of time.) Affective response is as essential an aspect of our humanness as is our sexuality. We have to be affective to be human.

We might ask what we should do with our genital sexual reactions, for being celibate must have a positive value and not be simply a condition of our work. Some clergy and religious use their celibacy as an excuse for avoiding intimacy. Some of these men and women even have genital relations and still avoid intimacy. They exhibit a typical pattern of genital contact, repentance, breaking up with the other, renewing commitment to vocation, and then genital involvement with yet another. Whether acknowledged or not, such involvement is intentional. The celibate is acting out an emotional or sexual problem.

Chastity is a difficult virtue for all of us. We must be realistic about our sexuality. We must not fear it, but we should acknowledge our individual fragility. Close friends must intend to remain celibate (chaste). They need to know that they want male-female intentional friendship, not a marital or quasi-marital relationship—not coupling. Something besides the relationship must be at the center of the friends' hearts. If one or the other friend or both experience a desire for sexual expression, the friends know that every desire need not be acted upon. If problems arise, the two must be open about the relationship. Being secretive creates a seductive atmosphere. Rash judgments from fellow celibates can encourage secretiveness. The relationship should be kept in the open so it can be understood by the community. Because our cultural value system is in such a state of change and because so many persons have left ministry, we tend to pull back and to grasp any safe way of living and dealing with the issues. Without real support systems, we turn a need for healthy privacy and growth into secrecy. We tend to support those who behave as we do and to criticize those who do not. It is difficult to support someone who is risking and struggling in a relationship of which we do not approve. Yet lack of support from others is one reason why we fail to communicate and to be open about our relationships.

All of us must cultivate a giving self and a receiving self. I love you because you are you and I am I, and it is good for us to be ourselves together. We need to develop the androgynous center of our being, our animus-masculine and anima-feminine qualities.

Different types of friendship

We must understand the confusion about the meaning of friendship today if we are to develop real friendships, intentional friendships. We need to know the dangers that can weaken, pervert, or transform our friendships into some other kind of relationship. For instance, Dale Carnegie's advice that we can make more friends in two months by becoming interested in other people than we can in two years by trying to get other people interested in us suggests that we can make true friends almost instantly. Carnegie also recommends telling people only what they want to hear. This advice confuses friends with admirers or fans. Making friends requires time and truth.

Often we do not distinguish among fans, collaborators, friendly acquaintances, pals, and true friends. Sometimes we assume that a friend is someone who knows us and still likes us. This assumption reduces a complex relationship to what is an occasional feeling and distorts our awareness of the full reality. At other times we identify a friend as one who satisfies our needs. But another person is greater than his or her usefulness to us. We take more than the person has to offer: we meet the person for who he or she is.

Aristotle distinguished three types of relationships that we generally regard as friendships. The first is friendship based on utility, which is sustained as long as the relationship proves to be useful. The second is friendship founded on pleasure, which disintegrates when one party is no longer entertained or amused by the other. The third kind of friendship exists between good people who are alike in excellence or virtue. Aristotle maintained that the first two types of friendship can be enjoyed, but should not be accepted as substitutes for true friendship. We should recognize that many of the people we name as friends are simply people we enjoy, or enjoy using, or who provide occasional companionship to help us avoid loneliness. I agree with Aristotle that there is a third kind of relationship called friendship, and I believe that it is essentially a form of love.

The love of friendship

Love is neither a special kind of feeling (*eros,* affection, or gratification of a felt need) nor a particular kind of concern or action, but a special kind of relationship between two persons. Two individuals within the bond of love discover and realize both their oneness and their freedom. Two persons become one, but are sustained as two persons. They affirm each other. To regard love from the viewpoint of one individual is to distort it. There is much emphasis, particularly in theological literature, on the unitive power of love. Too often the creative power of love is overlooked. We celibates can be cocreators. Love is an interpersonal relationship that can develop the best in persons and enable them to formulate appropriate identities, discover new dimensions of freedom, develop mature and responsible consciences, and give shape to hopeful, human worlds. Love is not just a special kind of feeling found in erotic or romantic natures or a merging of two personalities into one. It is an indispensable factor in personal growth toward full maturity.

When we love, we experience mutual trust; we feel free to relax and be ourselves. We feel at home with another person; we feel that we belong. Those who experience romantic and marital love are liberated from isolation so that they discover the freedom to be one. We who choose intentional friendship form a bond that allows us the freedom to be two. The danger is that one of us may assert dominance over the other or that we both may idolize our union so that it blinds us to the rest of reality, so that we share infatuation instead of love.

The Greeks invented a special word for friendship love, *philia*. Aristotle said of true *philia* that no one would choose to live without friends even if that person had all other goods. Friendship is an end in itself: to be a good friend, one must be morally good. To become a good friend, one must be another's equal and prove oneself worthy of friendship. Aristotle also saw love as an extension of self-love: "A man [sic] is his own best friend. . . . Therefore he [sic] should have the greatest affection for himself." Aristotle identified the highest form of friendship as the love of wisdom, whereby one is alone, contemplating truth known through the mind, but ignoring the truth known in the heart. I disagree, for Christ taught us that we must listen to the truth known in the heart.

Speaking to his apostles as friends, Christ emphasized their freedom. He told them that they would know the truth, and that the truth would set them free. Through loving one another, we experience mutual indwelling. We also are willing to sacrifice, suffer, and even die for our friends.

Thomas Aquinas affirmed that when we love another person, the good we seek is not our own but the good of our friend, for the friend's sake. When we love, we strive for insight into the friend's soul, so that our relationship can be characterized by knowledge as well as good will and affection.

Dante also celebrated the love of friendship. Virgil is Dante's friend who affirms his dignity and freedom. The most horrible punishment inflicted upon any of the damned in the *Inferno* is for betraying the bond of friendship.

During the Reformation, Luther and Calvin undermined the faith in human nature that is essential for the development of friendship by stressing the corruption of human nature. What mattered to them was what goes on between the believer and God. They made no room for the concept of love as a relationship between friends. The subsequent Protestant work ethic left no time to develop and enjoy close friendships.[2] In modern society, working relationships have become more important than personal relationships, and I-thou relationships have been overwhelmed with I-it attitudes. The value placed on success has led to an emphasis on individual achievement; keeping busy; lucrative productivity; effective manipulation of data, programs, and personnel; exotic experiences; and security of moral certainty that in our striving we are doing what is right. In addition, our geographical mobility deters friends from spending time together enjoying each other.

Characteristics of healthy friendship

We must appreciate what it means to have and to be a true friend if we are to develop a humane and hopeful world. William A. Sadler, Jr. identifies five characteristics of healthy friendship:[3]

1. *Joy.* When good friends meet, especially if they have been separated for some time, they share a special kind of happiness that we rightly identify as joy. Friends are delighted to see each other and to relax in the enjoyment of each other's presence. They will laugh easily and frequently and are willing to share their joy with others, to enlarge the circle of friends. Friends also feel contentment when they share a meaningful experience. If they are unable to share such an experience, they realize that the experience would have been even more meaningful if they had been able to share it.

2. *Communion.* Friends know that their relationship is held together by more than an equal satisfying of each other's needs. They know that their bond is sharing life's more meaningful moments, its suffering and struggles, its triumph and elation. Friends develop a sense of communion when they pursue a common interest, when they cooperate and share responsibilities in a project, or when they simply play. They need not have identical interests. After a long separation, friends who were once very close may find that their friendship has changed. This change occurs because the friends have not sustained a common life. They can renew or rebuild the friendship by establishing communion.

One way to establish communion is to engage in intimate conversation. Close friends can express their convictions, their worries, and their deepest questions to one another; they can also relate their most secret experiences because they trust each other. Whereas sexual intercourse is the consummation of romantic love, heart-to-heart conversation is the consummation of friendship. Both actions are personally fulfilling only if both persons seek to know who the other is.

Communion requires attentiveness, openness, and gentle sensitivity. We all experience loneliness, the feeling of being in a world where we are homeless. Loneliness is different from solitude, which is time lived quietly, contentedly alone, thinking, reading, looking, or listening. We should learn to enjoy solitude and to resist the temptations of loneliness. Rather than sense that people are essentially isolated from one another, we can sense a developing consciousness of our singular identity, in its distance from the environment and humanity in general. Friends can assure us of this identity, but we must not ask them to protect us from loneliness. If we do so, our friends become objects that satisfy our need for companionship. Friendship bestows communion that enables us to face loneliness with courage and the awareness that we are not totally alone in our world.

3. *Freedom.* The work of love is creative: it strengthens and liberates the individuals who love. If love is genuinely creative, then when we are loved we are changed, and we should expect those we love to have new strengths, new interests, and a keen appetite to pursue those interests. Love must be open to the other and be for the development of the other. It must also be ready for constant readjustment to the growth of the other.

Discovery is another gift of love. We will experience moments of surprise and discovery as newly emergent aspects of the other's personality become manifest. Such discovery is often a testimony to the liberating effect of love. Encouraged by friendship, persons will tend to exercise their freedom in the direction of personal development, expanding their horizons and actualizing latent potentialities.

Anxiety makes us uncertain and afraid, but a good friend provides us with feelings of worth and trust. When we are anxious or discouraged, we are apt to lose faith in others, in the environment, and in ourselves. We cannot open up and give ourselves to new possibilities. But when friends express faith in us, we are freed from some of the crippling effects of anxiety, for our friends accept us as we are. With our friends we do not have to compete to prove ourselves better than we really are. Yet if a friend's faith is genuine, it is not blind. If our friends pretend that our misdeeds do not exist, or if they ignore the facts of some of our foolish, selfish actions, then they do not really know us. If they acknowledge a wrong action and yet have faith in us, they will not condemn us but will know us as we are.

Forgiveness is an essential part of friendship, and Jesus was one of the first to express this truth. To be a friend means that we meet our friends not only with faith that affirms their freedom, but with forgiveness that releases them from a guilt that would inhibit their human action. Our freedom extends only as far as the horizon of our personal world. As we participate in the worlds of others, the size of our personal world increases. Thus an increase of freedom through faith, forgiveness, and mutual sharing in an interpersonal world that enlarges our own horizons is an essential element in friendship.

4. *Truth.* In friendship we speak of truth. Our friends may tell us that what we intend to do is inconsistent with our best purposes and character. They may tell us that what we have done is wrong. Their voices are our second conscience, based on an understanding of us and our situation that is both objective and sympathetic. We are fortunate if we have friends to help us reach our important decisions. A friend's judgment, honestly rendered and sympathetically expressed, can free us from self-deception, for the judgment is truth spoken in love. Friends not only encourage each other to be true to themselves and to each other, but also to live consistently with their truth when meeting social responsibilities. In particular, friendship encourages us to transform this world into the kind of place in which the values of friendship, such as love, freedom, and truth, will be honored.

As friends speak to us in truth, they help us to become aware of the persons that we are and might become. They help us sense our identities as whole persons. When we speak the truth to our friends, we discover a true vision of life and its possibilities.

5. *Sacrifice.* To share in another's life, we must be willing to sacrifice and suffer. Whenever we become involved with another person whose identity and freedom it is important for us to affirm, we must be prepared to sacrifice self-assertion and selfishness. To respond to a friend's call, we must say no, at least momentarily, to interests, plans, and activities that are important to us. This surrender is not a loss but an expression of freedom for the sake of our friends and our friendships. To have communion with friends, we must sacrifice some of our aggressive tendencies and peculiar desires or genital stirrings. When we love, both joy and suffering may be conditions of our relationship.

These characteristics constitute a skeleton of friendship, the proportions of which will differ as friends and friendships differ. The relationships that priests and religious develop are often service-oriented and functional without ever becoming deeply personal. Yet it is only through deep personal relationships that we come to know ourselves as we really are and learn to deal with our feelings honestly and maturely. After all, the call to celibacy is a call to become fully human by going ever deeper into life.

Falling in love

In the psychosexual development of life, everyone must go through the adolescent stage and experience infatuation. Many priests and religious who entered seminaries or novitiates at an early age, even during late adolescence (up to age twenty-seven), may not have experienced falling in love. Because they were no longer in contact with the opposite sex once they entered priestly or religious life, their growth was stunted. Thus priests and religious may find themselves falling in love at age forty or fifty. They will recognize it for what it is, and they may feel guilty, not because they have acted out physically, but because of their fantasies. The two involved in this friendship have to talk honestly and distance themselves. If an embrace evokes genital feelings, then it should be avoided.

No amount of personal commitment to an ideal of celibate chastity will automatically prevent a person from falling in love. When priests and religious recognize their real feelings of attraction and affection for another person, they may naturally feel guilty for having compromised their vows. These feelings flow from their background and training. We must therefore realize that most people fall in love a number of times in life and that what is important is how the experience of falling in love is dealt with and integrated into previous life commitments. In a friendship between a married layperson and a priest or religious, each person has a previous commitment—the layperson to the married partner, the priest or religious to God. Each one should respect the choice of the other. Our celibacy and our communities are part of who we are. The other loves this wholeness. We priests and religious would not be ourselves without it. In a healthy friendship, the married person who sees the priest or religious friend becoming estranged from commitment to God and community will remind the friend about the prior commitment. Fellow priests or religious should also invite the friend to look at his or her commitment. True friends love one another's wholeness. They help one another struggle with who each is, remembering who each has been in the past and who each had hoped to be in the future. If friends use this suffering as an opportunity to offer oneness elsewhere, with each other, they are no longer friends.

We cannot condemn people for their feelings. The fascination of coupling can become intense, particularly among priests and religious who never experienced the normal adolescent infatuation that is part of our emotional development. But true intentional friendship means more than one friend. The celibate should have many friends, for multiple friendship is one way in which coupling and intentional friendship differ. There will be times when friends are no longer present. But the memory of friendships and the growth they brought us will always remain. These memories and our relationship with Christ will sustain us.

The following comments can serve as guidelines for male-female relationships in general and for celibate-layperson and celibate-celibate relationships in particular.

1. Both persons need a high degree of self-knowledge. Immature persons are often very clumsy in developing such relationships. Self-knowledge is most important.

2. The persons must be selective about the individuals with whom they form a special friendship. Do not seek friendships with unhappy persons. Friendships should be between persons happy with their lives, their lifestyles, and their deliberate life choices.

3. Relationships must be consistent with a person's celibate commitment and lifestyle.

4. Caution signs include: erotic manifestations, resentment when others are present, demanding responses such as "drop everything and everyone and be present to me," community or rectory life suffering because of a one-to-one relationship, and relationships that lead to an erosion of interior prayer and spiritual realities.

Friendships enable us to become simultaneously aware of our riches and our poverty. We are not long in realizing that what we possess is far inferior to what we would like to give our friends. We must therefore continue to grow, and in large part it will be the generosity of our friends that will enable us to increase our riches, both on the level of having and on the level of being. True friendship is possible only when we recognize and accept the differences that distinguish us from others. By making ourselves more available to others, we become more and more ourselves. In friendship we discover and reveal what we are and, perhaps still more, what we are capable of becoming. It is normal for friends to influence one another. But when we influence our friends, we need not communicate our own riches; rather we should help our friends discover their own riches. This is the greatest gift we can give to others. It follows then that friendship demands discretion, disinterest and forgetfulness of self, and renunciation of inordinate self-love.

Whatever the dangers, it is my firm conviction that friendship between celibate men and women is not an impossible ideal. But it can be realized only between persons who have attained a relatively high degree of spirituality and whose higher values are very much in evidence.

Moreover, friendship does not necessarily last forever. We will lose friends through death and prolonged physical separation. Other persons may come between us, or our friends may betray us. Everything human is fragile, the degree of fragility depending upon the individuals and their situations. Persons sharing even the most beautiful friendships often have an obscure feeling that they are not understood and loved absolutely. Yet, despite its imperfections and limitations, friendship is one of the most precious values of the human condition.

Belonging to our friends and to God

Still, because of its limitations, friendship will never fully satisfy the human heart. As Augustine said, "You have made our hearts for you, O God, and they are restless until they rest in you." All that I have said about the value of human friendship should be applied to our friendship with God. Joy, communion, truth, freedom, and sacrifice are inherent in our friendship with God. There will be times in our lives when we have only God. For that reason, we must develop a deep life of prayer that must be worked at, just as every human relationship must be worked at. The mystery of the human beings with whom we are friends can become our basis for approaching the mystery of God. The reality of God can be described as a mysterious shared goal of friends. So celibate friendship can contribute to a vision of God as the ultimate mystery of love, sometimes present and sometimes absent, always moving toward a very personal love, to be sought as the common goal and hope of life. The process of becoming will lead to belonging. We cannot be detached if we have not known attachment. In turn, integrating this non-possessiveness brings not only personal benefits to those involved, but enrichment to the whole Church and the world by its witness to mystery, love, and hope in God. Thus we celibates can be this model for friendship. Our sense of longing to be becomes a belonging both to our friends and to God.

Endnotes

1. Johann Michele Rake, "Friendship: A Fundamental Description," *Humanitas* 6 (Fall 1970): 175.

2. I am greatly indebted to William A. Sadler, Jr., "The Experience of Friendship," *Humanitas* 6 (Fall 1970): 177-209, for the above discussion of Aristotle and others.

3. Ibid., pp. 197-208.

II.

Women in the Adventure of Affirming

Chapter Four

From loneliness to holiness

$\mathcal{T}$he existential experience of loneliness can lead us to a solitude of soul whereby we become whole and holy, whereby we learn what it means to "be still and know that I am God" (Psalms 46:10). While experiencing existential loneliness, we ceaselessly question ourselves, others, our world, and even our God, demanding significant answers that make a lasting impact on our lives. Our questioning offers us the opportunity to discover and then know ourselves, our relation to others and to God, and our place in our world. Through an apparent breakdown of meaning, we find real meaning. We realize that by learning to be alone with ourselves we learn to be with and for others, that in the solitude of soul found in loneliness we discover the threads that bind the human community, and that by first moving away from others we encounter our real selves and God and are then able to move more genuinely toward others.

When I was asked many months ago to speak at this symposium, I intended to write a treatise to develop the thesis expressed above. For weeks my mind was filled with ideas for this treatise and with worries about its completion. Books and notes began to cover my desk; wads of crumpled and discarded papers became scattered about my office. I began to feel crowded, as if there were no room for me. I began feeling lonely. Then last night, I attended the performance of a drama that expressed all I had to say about loneliness to holiness with more clarity, immediacy, and eloquence than I could ever hope to convey.

The Adventure of Affirming

Having for weeks been crowded into an intellectual corner, smothered by abstract words and ideas, frustrated by my inability to breathe life into these abstractions even while polishing my text, I suddenly was experiencing—seeing, hearing, feeling—my thesis. The performance was the intellectual expression of my ideas given a physical and spiritual dimension. Actually moved to tears, I knew that those attending the symposium should share this lived experience. I knew that this performance, not my text, was the essence of our experience of loneliness to holiness.

When last night Sister Eileen Horan, R.S.M., first performed her interpretive dance and monologue, she had no idea she would be performing it again today at the symposium. For the last two years, we at the House of Affirmation have wanted to invite all former residents of the House to return for a weekend. Because this year the third anniversary of the founding of the House on the Feast of St. Therese, October 1, 1973, coincides with my Silver Jubilee on October 3, we decided to extend the invitation to our former residents for this weekend and to schedule the symposium today, October 2. We have always held the symposium in conjunction with the founding, but this year we hoped that all former residents would attend the symposium and join with our current residents to help us celebrate both the founding of the House and my twenty-five years of religious profession. Sister Eileen's performance last night at the House was in honor of this celebration.

Sister Eileen knows the House well. She was a resident there for many months about two years ago, and I was her therapist. A Sister of Mercy of Rhode Island, she received her master's degree in drama from Emerson College, Boston.

Her dramatic talents are many, to which her performance will attest. But more important, Sister Eileen's performance attests to her having traveled the road from loneliness to holiness. In psychotherapy, Sister Eileen encountered her loneliness and let it lead her (admittedly only after much struggle) to that solitude of soul whereby we become whole and holy. She has thanked me (her drama is entitled *Gratiae Tante, Anna*) for having helped her along the way, for having given her new life and new hope. I was able to help because I too have encountered loneliness. I too have explored the depths of solitude and emerged more whole and holy. By listening to the language of loneliness, I became sensitive to myself and to others. Obviously, Sister Eileen has become similarly sensitive. Alone with my treatise, my approach to it exacerbated my loneliness. Sister Eileen's drama was a reminder. Just as in therapy my acceptance, understanding, and concern had given her the courage to confront her loneliness, so her drama gave me the opportunity to recover myself. Sister Eileen's dramatic path from loneliness to holiness is my path and your path and the path of all human beings who finally approach their loneliness creatively.

Yet I do not mean to imply that the road from loneliness to holiness is ever easy; Sister Eileen's path was labyrinthine, beset not only with loneliness but depression, anxiety, guilt, frustration, anger, and much psychic anguish, more than many of us can imagine, and much more than most of us will ever experience. When Sister Eileen began therapy, she was silent for more than three months. Yet I knew intuitively what she was experiencing. She communicated with me through her silence. I patiently waited for her to speak. As her therapy progressed, she revealed to me the depths of her soul. Her soul spoke to my soul. Now as you watch and listen to her drama, her soul will speak to your soul as well. Sister Eileen will tell you what it means to experience existential loneliness, and you will know why I could not resist asking her to share with you what she has shared with me. Sister Eileen's very presence here, her public performance, attests to the great distance she has traveled on her road from loneliness to holiness since her months of silence two years ago. She wrote most of the words, developed the choreography, and chose the music for her drama. She is assisted by Reverend John Fitzgerald, another former resident of the House who has served as her technical advisor.

[The script of Sister Eileen's drama follows, punctuated by short commentaries by Sister Anna Polcino, M.D.]

GRATIAE TANTE, ANNA

A drama created in honor of and to thank Sister Anna Polcino, M.D., and dedicated to her, to all the former and present residents and staff, both clinical and nonclinical, of the House of Affirmation, and to the members of my own community, the Sisters of Mercy of Rhode Island, for their love, their support, and their concern as I have searched and as I continue to search today for God's will in my life.

I. Who Controls Me?
Music: "A Fifth of Beethoven"
Walter Murphy and the Big Apple Band

Although Sister Eileen remained silent during much of her early therapy, I knew she was questioning her own identity. In the depths of loneliness we each ask the question: who am I? In this section of her drama, Sister Eileen conveys the destructive effect of incessant change on our lives and of our resultant tendency to assume many identities, none of which is our own. Each time we have established a rhythm, a beat, by which we can cope with and adapt ourselves to one stimulus, we are confronted by another. Each time we think we know who we are, we are asked to be someone else. Eventually, unable to adapt to ever-increasing changes in the beat of our lives, we lose control. No longer sure of even our identity, we have no foundation upon which to build change, no pivot upon which to revolve. We are no longer able to integrate the stimuli that barrage us from every direction. In our attempts to be everyone, we are no one. Sister Eileen asks, "Who's in control?" She knows she is not, and she wonders if she can trust anyone to be so. Can she trust her therapist? She fears trust as much as she fears change; she fears loss of control of her own impulses; she feels threatened. Finally, although still unsure, still anxious, she reaches out to her therapist, admitting her loss of identity, her loss of control, and her willingness to trust her therapist to help her find herself. The therapist becomes a significant other who helps her to admit and affirm both what she is and what she is experiencing.

Who controls me?
Who controls my being me?
Who controls me?
Who controls my being me?[1]
Who am I?
Who are you?
Who are we?
Who are they?
Who am I?
Who are you?
Who are we?
Who are they?
Who's in control? Who's in control?
Control?
NO!
There's only change, further change, more change
Update
Innovate
Renovate
Amalgamate
Disintegrate
Reinstate
Limitate
Accommodate
Re-order
Re-structure
Start again
Where's the direction? Where's my place?
Only change, further change, more change.
Control?

Who's in control?
It's not I.
Hey, I'll play the part, o-o-o-oh, ye-h-h-h
Tell me of the mask to wear.
Move with the image, baby.
This is the way you see me.
Maybe that's what I am.

The Adventure of Affirming

Check the way I move, babe.
Check the way I stand.
I'll play your image to the hilt
If that's what you want to see.
I can be most anything, just give me to the count of three.
Stay with the rhythm, move with the beat.
Mesmerized, hypnotized
Stay with the rhythm, move with the beat.
Mesmerized, hypnotized
This is the way I cope, friend, this is the way I cope.
Stay with the rhythm, move with the beat.
Then I control reality.
Change, change, no, don't change.
Change, change, no, don't change the beat.
Change, change, no, don't change.
Change, change, no, don't change the beat.
Don't threaten me.
Who changed the rhythm?
Who changed the beat?
Where's the set identity?
Who changed the rhythm?
Who changed the beat?
Where's the set identity?
Exploration, no.
Encounter, no.
Search, no.
Adventure, no.
Choose, no.
Respond, I can't.
Why the change?
Who's in control?
I've lost control.
Let me just move with the beat, man.
Let me just move with the beat.
Uncertainty
Insecurity
Lost ability
No identity
Choose fantasy
Deny reality
Oh, the change, further change, more change
Who's in control?
I've lost control.

Help me.
Hold me.
Heal me.
Yess-ss-ss-ss-sss
Liberate me.

II. That's Life?   *No music*

Disjunct thought, nursery rhymes, and machine-like repetition characterize this section where Sister Eileen conveys what modern technology does to our creative approach to life. She questions whether life has meaning if in order to survive we must become dehumanized automatons that respond to any and every stimulus, including inane appeals to purchase products advertised on television. Her therapy has given her hope "of being fully alive," creatively and humanly alive, but the "powerful beat" of "incessant change" and "constant yet subtle oppression of the mind's creative adaptation to life" make her wonder whether to fit in she must despair of ever knowing and controlling her own self. Her therapist has told her that she must risk in order to know. But she fears coming into contact with her own aggression, hostility, ambivalence, or general incompleteness with its attendant human shortcomings. Shouldn't she take the "safer path" and repeat the beat? Yet still hopeful, she embraces the "new way of thinking" called assertion.

Liberate me.
Help me.
Hold me.
Heal me.
Liberate me from the bonds of my own slavery,
        from the chains of my own thought,
        from the shackles I've learned were not of my making.
I want to do certain things,
        be certain things,
        say certain things,
        love certain people and be loved by them.
I want to believe that I have a unique contribution to make to this
        world and that I cannot be truly myself unless I am able to
        make it. Unless I can truly love for all I'm worth, then I
        shall not care to be alive.

The Adventure of Affirming

Alive?
Me?
Full of life?
Oh-h-h-h
Just the image of being fully alive; it makes me want to hope,
Really hope.
But, sometimes, I look out there, way out there,
And I say,
That's life? Life?
On the one hand, incessant change demanding an ongoing, never-
ending adjustment. And on the other, a constant yet subtle
oppression of the mind's creative adaptation to life by means
of a battery of artificial standards and goals.

Life.
That's life?
Life?
For the rhythm of life has a powerful beat.
For the rhythm of life has a powerful beat.
For the rhythm of life has a powerful beat.
Repeat, repeat, repeat, repeat.
Repeat, repeat, repeat, repeat.
"Kelloggs, because your best days start with breakfast."
"Bayer, for the kind of relief you can't get from an aspirin sub-
stitute."
"A & P, if we can't do it, nobody can."
"NBC sends you all the best."
Repeat, repeat, repeat, repeat.
Repeat, repeat, repeat, repeat.
Step the step, play the role.
Step the step, play the role.
All I have to do is fit in, right?
All I have to do is fit in.
Just a cog in the wheel
Just a cog in the wheel
Technology, Mass-s-s-s production
Technology, Mass-s-s-s production
All I have to do is fit in, right?
All I have to do is fit in.
One, two, buckle ma shoe.
Three, four, shut de door.
Five, six, pick up sticks.
Seven, eight, lay dem straight.
Repeat, repeat, repeat, repeat.

All I have to do is fit in, right?
All I have to do is fit in.
Mary had a little lamb.
It's fle-e-ece was whi-i-ite as sno-o-ow.
And everywhere that Mary went,
That damn lamb was sure to go.
All I have to do is fit in, right?
All I have to do is fit in.
Pease porridge hot, pease porridge cold,
Pease porridge in the pot nine days old.
All I have to do is fit in, right?
All I have to do is fit in.
Mistress Mary, quite contrary,
How does your garden grow?
With silver bells and cockleshells
And pretty maids all in a row.
All in a row
All in a row
All in a row
All in a row
Repeat, repeat, repeat, repeat.
Technology, mass-s-s-s production
Technology, mass-s-s-s production
Tell me what to eat.
Tell me what to wear.
Tell me where to go
And tell me how to get there.
Tell me what to eat.
Tell me what to wear.
Tell me where to go
And tell me how to get there.
All I have to do is fit in, right?
Do I really want a place in the history of man?
Have we ever truly gained a new understanding of ourselves?
So much oppression
Both obvious and subtle
And so much revolution
I too revolt.
I struggle to be free.
Oh, not to subdue again,
Not to oppress another in any form,
But only to change, to grow,
To learn to live with my own incompleteness
And to let that incompleteness

Help me become one with the created order of the entire universe,
And thus move toward identity.
Oh, God, I hate to repeat, repeat.
But I fear working with that which is incomplete.
'Tis almost better,
'Tis so much safer to
Repeat, repeat, repeat, repeat
The safe path, the safe path.
Risk? Risk?
You want me to risk?
Revolve toward that which is most natural in all of us?
Recover my relationship with the world and with my god?
Risk, huh?
Risk, r . . . i . . . s . . . k
"Throw it off.
Cast it aside.
Put on the new man."[2]
Put on the new man.
Put on the new man.
Yeh?
Yeh Yeh-h-h. Y-E-H-H-H-H!
There's a new way of thinking.
There's a new way of thinking.
There's a new way of thinking.
It's gonna put me in motion.
There's a new way of thinking.
There's a new way of thinking.
There's a new way of thinking.
And it's called AS-SERTION!

III. Capisce?

Music: "Boogie-Woogie"
Roper Dance Orchestra
Roper Records

Therapy has taught Sister Eileen not to "play it safe," not to
deny but to affirm and appreciate herself and her experiences.
Significant others, her therapist, and the members of the staff
and residential community at the House of Affirmation, have
allowed her to be, to evolve, to work herself out; they have offered her acceptance and support. But in this section, Sister
Eileen reveals her continuing fear. She has begun to discover

what she is and wants rather than what society wants her to be, but her discovery has made her feel angry, embarrassed, and foolish. She begs to retreat. Her new-found assertion waxes and wanes. She asks herself, as her therapist has asked: "Capisce (do you understand)?" She has begun to understand, and here she concludes "assertion's the name of the game." But is the "game" any different from the "powerful beat"? Sister Eileen ponders this question in the next section and shares her great discovery with us.

ASSERT

Grab on to learning the most direct
For greater expression of affect.
Experiment and try new roles.
Don't play it safe with your head in a hole.
Don't rationalize,
And don't deny,
And never project,
But always reply.
O-o-o-o-o-oh, yeh.
Assert, assert
Assert, assert
Assert, assert
Oh, retreat, retreat
Please let me retreat.
Oh, let me retreat.
Express myself and be most firm.
Sometimes I think I'll never learn
Assertion's the name of this game.
Others are worth far more than I;
Their right to say no is greater than mine.
I've heard nice people never say no.
And since I'm a doll, how could it be so?
Redeem me from the incessant yes
And move me toward the salvific no.
O-o-o-o-o-oh, yeh!
Don't bother me, I can't cope.
Assertion's now my only hope.
I'll not back down.
You're out of line.
I'll go where you want,
Oh, no I won't.

The Adventure of Affirming

This dress is too tight,
And it's rather short.
Don't bother to flirt;
It just doesn't work.
I'd like a raise
For the work I do.
Don't get the idea
I can't handle you.
No, I don't want any brooms today.
Oh, help my efforts to turn them away.
O-o-o-o-o-oh, yeh!
Oh, assertion
Dear assertion
Bless assertion
Yeh, assertion
Oh, assertion
Dear assertion
Bless assertion
Yeh, assertion
Prepare my script;
Write down my lines;
Observe my cues;
Hit them on time.
Oh, yes, I do have feelings today;
The things you drop are in my way;
Hold it on the salt if you please;
Hand me the pepper, I'd rather sneeze.
Bless my attempts at mastery.
Remove from me all futility.
I'm not Bo-Peep;
I've lost no sheep.
I'll not pretend to tolerate.
There's nothing now I'll mitigate.
Grab on to learning the most direct
For greater expression of affect.
Experiment and try new roles.
Don't play it safe with your head in a hole.
Don't rationalize,
And don't deny,
And never project,
But always reply.
O-o-o-o-o-oh, yeh!
Assert, assert
Assert, assert

Assert, assert
Capisce, capisce
Assert, assert
Capisce, capisce
Express myself and be most firm.
Sometimes I think I'll never learn.
Assertion's the name of the game.
Yeah!

IV. Beneath the Surface   *No music*

The "game" and the "powerful beat" are surface realities, necessary to life, but not its essential meaning, which is found beneath the surface, "down deep, where you hurt and where I hurt, and where we both rejoice," where "it's not a game at all." At life's core abides the deeper, more meaningful reality, whose truth can speak to us only when we are still, only in silence. Here "immersed," we experience that solitude of soul whereby we become whole and holy. But Sister Eileen's discovery of this truth is fleeting. She cannot sustain her solitude as others have done whose solitude "clothes their nakedness with love." Her brief encounter with solitude leads again to loneliness—"no one"—which "strips [her] with the anguish of self-doubt and the absolute death of self-hate." But she persists; she plunges to the depths again, knowing she must "live," "feel," and "be torn by" her "intolerable loneliness" in order to emerge from it with a solitude of soul whereby "there shall be one." Yet repeatedly, at life's core, "as it was in the beginning," she finds only the unhealthy silence of her early days of therapy. She is unable to restore her glimpse of the stillness of solitude that speaks of the Word. She encounters "the rub" of loneliness, but she never loses hope of again being still and knowing God.

The game
Oh, yeh!
The game, the great big game
Only down deep,
Way down deep,
Where you hurt and where I hurt,

And where we both rejoice,
It's not a game at all.
It's life.
It's life,
And it says yes,
And it says no,
And it says come,
And it says let go.
But most of all,
Most of all,
It says be still,
        be still.
"Teach us to care and not to care,
And teach us to sit still."[3]
For if we do not understand your silence,
We shall never understand your words.
For the rhythm of life has a powerful beat.
For the rhythm of life has a powerful beat.
For the rhythm of life has a powerful beat.
Be still!
Be still!
Immersion in the stillness is immersion in the mystery
Is immersion in the Word, and the Word is Truth?
Be still!
Be still.
Oh,
But when I'm still,
When I am fully and totally alone,
Immersed in solitude,
Then so often
There is the deepest collision
"between my tormenting and my tormented self."[4]
God, "I'm up to Heaven and down to Hell in an hour."[5]
For others,
Their solitude clothes their nakedness with love.
but mine, mine strips me with the anguish of self-doubt and the
        absolute death of self-hate.
Stillness?
Emptiness.
Loneliness!
No . . . One
No one!
No one.
No-o-o-o

No-o-o-o
Live with the no one.
Feel the no one.
Be torn by the no one,
And there shall be one.
There shall be one?
"The voice of love makes an emptiness and a solitude reverberate."[6]
The voice of love?
There shall be one?
"I will lead her into the wilderness and I will speak to her heart."[7]
There is only wilderness.
There is no word!
There shall be one?
In this intolerable loneliness, there shall be one?
As it was in the beginning?
Oh, there's the rub.
There's the rub.
As it was in the beginning . . .

V. The Ultimate Prayer

Music: Prelude in C sharp minor
Rachmaninoff
Van Cliburn

In loneliness our experience of time and space changes. We begin to look back at the past and relate the present and future to the past. Sister Eileen's hope of hearing the Word "as it was in the beginning" has caused her to ponder not only the beginning of her therapy, but the beginning of her life, from birth onward. She is aware of never having been touched by love, never having had her being affirmed by a significant other. She has been denied to such an extent that she has had "to pretend," "to choose . . . one thousand masks" in order to secure an identity. She admits: "I think I am,/But I am not." Unloved, unaffirmed, she has been "deeply wounded," suffering "great fear," "enormous guilt," "tormenting anxiety," and "much anticipation of total rejection." Life has been a series of "games," of "powerful beats" that she now describes as "ever-spinning, whirling circles" that push, pull, and pressure her to accommodate and assimilate

67

change at a pace that is different from her own. Growing outwardly into an adult, a woman religious, she has remained inwardly a child, her growth stunted by the absence of love and the acceptance integral to it. Uncomprehending, she runs from herself, fearing the reality within her and fearing even more that there may be no reality. She yearns for the healing touch of affirmation, the "hand" of the "healer" for whom she will wait and to whom she will give her trust.

> "Every first thing continues forever with the child:
> the first color, the first music, the first flower paint
> the foreground of his [sic] life. The first inner and
> outer object of love, injustice, or such like throws a
> shadow immeasurably far along his after years."[8]

And so it begins.
My life begins.
At least I think it's life.
And I move,
And I perform,
And I reach out,
And I do all that I hope will allow love to touch me.
But it touches me not,
Not fully, not deeply.
And I think I am,
But I am not.
So full of empty spaces,
Of stark desert places.
For "what I say, I don't feel.
And what I feel, I don't show.
And what I show isn't real.
What is real, Lord, I don't know."[9]
And so I remain small
And deeply wounded
And terribly angry but know it not.
And so I learn to pretend
And to choose the one thousand masks that will secure me.
But with great fear
And enormous guilt
And tormenting anxiety
And so much anticipation of total rejection.
Yes, the desperate, pretending games
That hold the captive, trembling child within.

So much so
That all I know are circles,
Ever-spinning, whirling circles—
Up again around and down again around
And pulling and pushing and pressure, unbearable pressure.
To run, run
Don't stand still,
Don't look back,
For then you may know it as it really is.
And so I ran;
And so pretended,
In no way comprehending the Hell in my own life,
Forced to grow outwardly "with no voice for the infant cries and
          rages."[10]
Yearning, burning to be touched
By a single, gentle hand.
"I need a way of seeing in the dark.
What way is this, what dark is this?"[11]
I need.
I need.
Is there no one?
"Whoever welcomes a child such as this welcomes me."[12]
No one?
"Free my soul from death,
        my eyes from tears,
        and my feet from stumbling."[13]
Say to me: "Ephphatha, be opened."
Am I not worthy of the touching?
Put your fingers into my ears
And, spitting, touch my tongue.
Say to me:
"Ephphatha, be opened
Ephphatha, be opened."[14]
Is there no hand?
Just one, to be His hand?
Is there no healer
To be His healer?
"And help me walk into the presence of the Lord, into the land of
          the living."[15]
No hand?
No healer?
"For you I wait all the day
And to you I give my trust unto safekeeping."[16]

VI. Her Name Was Anna

The therapist heals by affirming, by creating within her client a trust, an approval, an appreciation, and a reverence for who she is and who she can become. The therapist listens to her client's loneliness. Plumbing its inner depths together, the therapist and client emerge sharing that solitude of soul wherein all meaning lies. The therapist-healer serves as a guide, pointing the way to the ultimate Healer, to all that is and ever shall be. The therapist is ever a symbol of hope and renewal, a promise of psychological rebirth through the healing touch of affirmation, through the power of love. Affirmed herself, the therapist is able to be for others, never clinging, never possessing, always assisting the birth, careful to "clothe the child in love and trust/And then give it over to the calling of life itself when it is life's time."

INTRODUCTION   *No music*

And so I waited,
As we all have waited,
Knowing that we must have love
Even if there is no more of it in this world,
Knowing that the solitary agony of Christ
Is the agony of us all at certain moments.
Waiting,
Waiting for the one
Whose hand would be that of the Healer.

> Music: *"Nadia's Theme"*
> *Perry Botkin, Jr.*
> *from "Bless the Beasts and the Children"*

And then the Father sent her.
Her name was Anna.
And to her I gave my trust
And laid bare the depths of my soul.
For you, Anna, are one
Whose hope is strong.
"You see and cherish all signs of life
And are truly ready at every moment
to help the birth of that which is ready to be born."[17]
Everyone of us here
And so many who are distant

Have been nourished by the immensity of your love
And the humaneness of your being.
"In you, hope never ceases to surge up
And explore its own heights,
And your love,
Your love moves in a stillness to contemplate its own depths."[18]
You perform the most graceful healing, for you leave yourself
So exposed and vulnerable,
Letting the sore and wounded places within you
Reach out to tenderly touch another.[19]
Your beauty,
The radiance of the truth within you,
Never clings,
Never possesses.
You assist the birth,
Clothe the child in love and trust,
And then give it over to the calling of life itself when it is life's
        time.
And so we all pray to the Father in Heaven,
That He will bestow on you
Gifts in keeping with the riches of His glory.
May He strengthen you inwardly
Through the power of His Spirit.
May Christ always dwell in your heart through faith.
May love always be the root and foundation of your life.
And, Anna, may you experience always the fullness of God Him-
        self.[20]

I believe that after many years of suffering, Sister Eileen has received the fullness of God himself. Her drama traces the labyrinthine pathway the soul travels on its journey from loneliness to holiness. Impeded by the "powerful beat" of our culture which militates against a creative experience of loneliness, Sister Eileen felt only emptiness and senselessness. Whirling in circles, out of control, knowing only a repetitious rhythm, she asked herself why she was alive. In therapy, she was given the opportunity to experience creatively her loneliness, to confront and renew her life. As she worked through her psychological problems, God was present in the depths of her soul. Her loneliness was a prelude to a solitude of soul whereby she felt God's presence. She lived, felt, and was torn by the "no one" in order that there should be One whose Word would speak to her in the stillness of her solitude. By sharing her loneliness during therapy and during her performance yesterday and today, I too heard the Word and was renewed in my conviction that my purpose in life is to heal by affirming others so that they may experience the fullness of the Healer who is and ever shall be.

Endnotes

1. In this section and the one that follows, I am indebted to Reverend Thomas A. Kane for the ideas expressed in his books entitled *Who Controls Me?* (Hicksville, N. Y.: Exposition Press, 1974) and *The Healing Touch of Affirmation* (Whitinsville, Mass.: Affirmation Books, 1976).

2. Eph. 4:22-24. All biblical quotations are taken from *The Jerusalem Bible* (New York: Doubleday, 1966).

3. T. S. Eliot, "Ash Wednesday," *Selected Poems* (New York: Harcourt, Brace and World, 1964).

4. May Sarton, *Journal of a Solitude* (New York: Norton, 1973).

5. Ibid.

6. Francois Mauriac, *Journal d'un homme de 30 ans,* as quoted in Sarton.

7. Hos. 2:16.

8. Source unavailable.

9. Leonard Bernstein, *The Mass,* Columbia Records.

10. Sarton.

11. Peter Shaffer, *Equus* (New York: Avon Books, 1974).

12. Mark 9:37.

13. Ps. 116:8.

14. Mark 7:33-34.

15. Ps. 16.

16. Ps. 25.

17. Erich Fromm, *The Art of Loving* (New York: Harper and Row, 1956).

18. Lois Huffman, ed., *Whisperings: The Inspirational Writings of Tagore* (Kansas City, Mo.: Hallmark, 1973).

19. Bernard Bush, "Healing Grace," *The Way* (July, 1976): 189-98.

20. Eph. 3:16-17.

Chapter Five

Women and healing

*B*ecause I am both a woman and a physician, the role of the woman in the healing process is of particular interest to me. Unfortunately, many women believe that healing is the concern only of the medically sophisticated physician and that, because the great majority of women are not physicians, they therefore, need not and cannot participate in healing. But we must remember that healing is a spiritual, emotional, and intellectual, as well as a physical, process. In fact, one group of physicians of which I am a member—psychiatrists—has based its branch of medicine on this fact. Because healing is such a total process, it follows that society as a whole—all human beings, and therefore all women—can be healers, certainly not in a physical sense but most certainly in an emotional, intellectual, and spiritual sense.

Healing can be characterized as a lifelong response to life made by persons as individuals and as groups. Such a response allows us to participate in a creative process and to reach new levels of maturity. A healing response helps us enable others— our relatives, our loved ones, our friends, our neighbors, and even strangers—to meet the challenges of life. A healing response helps us as Christians to respond, in turn, to the Gospel message.

Women who respond as healers are following the example of Jesus, the divine physician, who healed humanity by affirming all persons and all things with whom he came in contact. Notice I use the word affirming. Women who respond as healers gain more and more insight into a role that has been of significance to them from the very first moment of creation. Women heal by affirming.

Affirmation is acceptance of the goodness of the other person to be as he or she is, immaturity and shortcomings notwithstanding. A healer does not expect others to measure up to preconceived standards; a healer allows others to be who they are not out of fear but out of free choice. A healer encourages other persons to be who they are so that they may realize their potential. Affirmation is like the sun beaming upon a rose. The rose can bloom and become delicately fragrant only if the sun shines on it, bringing it to maturity. In a similar manner, women who affirm other women, and women who affirm men, affirm all that is good in others.

The New Testament celebrates examples of Jesus' affirmation and healing. Jesus so much wanted his followers to be at peace, to take delight in him, to be thinkers of their thoughts, and feelers of their feelings rather than just doers. As a matter of fact, Jesus was repelled by the busyness of the people in his father's temple. He was repelled by the futility of all the "doing" rules of the Pharisees. Jesus went about healing wounds of anxiety, of unhappiness, of low self-esteem. I would like to encourage you to take up your Bible and reflect on the many ways in which the divine physician affirmed and thereby healed humanity, always with a tender, loving care.

Remember when Zacchaeus the tax collector was in a tree, neither loved nor accepted? Zacchaeus wanted to be accepted simply for being himself. He had never known such acceptance, and he evidently placed some hope in this Jesus of Nazareth. When Jesus was passing through the neighborhood, Zacchaeus knew Jesus would draw a crowd. So Zacchaeus, being short of stature, worked his way through the crowd and then climbed a sycamore tree at the side of the road. Jesus does not pass by Zacchaeus but accepts him as he is. Jesus calls out: "Zacchaeus, come down because I must stay with you today." Jesus affirms the little man in the tree. What is the result? Zacchaeus immediately unfolds like a flower in bloom. He replies to the Lord, "Here and now, I give away half of my possessions to charity, and, if I have cheated anyone, I am ready to repay four times over" (Luke 19:1-9).

Of course, other samples of the affirming Jesus abound in the New Testament. He affirmed a criminal next to him on the cross (Luke 23:39-43). He affirmed his mother, Mary, at the marriage feast of Cana (John 2:1-11). He affirmed the little children when his apostles were ready to turn them away (Mark 10:13-16). He affirmed the woman taken in adultery, choosing not to condemn her and telling her to go and sin no more (John 8:8-10). He affirmed Peter, giving him new strength and new concern, even though Peter had denied him three times (Matthew 16:16-20).

In all these acts, Jesus teaches us that the union of human persons creates an atmosphere for growth and healing. Jesus, whose body is the church, offers us the gift of being affirmed members of his body and thereby knowing a new dignity.

We women should recognize and take advantage of our opportunity to affirm humanity and to affirm all of God's creation by allowing people to be who they are meant to be and by creating the time and the space in life to encourage them to develop their potential. Our aim should be to foster the growth of each person by sharing with that person who we are, what we have, and what we do. We then become true followers of Christ to further the social, physical, mental, and spiritual development of the whole person. Everyone seeks wholeness. In our Western culture, men and women experience a lack of wholeness, a sense of brokenness that is in need of healing. If women themselves grow in affirmation and enable others to do likewise, they will be among the best healers of and in society.

Denial and affirmation

Not many years ago, the French philosopher and playwright, Gabriel Marcel, wrote a play entitled *Other People's*

Hearts, which depicts a marriage whose fundamental dynamics are those of denial, not affirmation. As the plot develops, the husband more and more considers his wife as part of himself, denying her individuality by assuming that she must think as he thinks and feel as he feels. The husband takes the wife for granted and presumes that his wishes are her wishes. He never discusses his plans with her or allows that she may have her own independent thoughts or opinions. The wife gradually begins to feel more and more that she is a thing used, not a person but a possession, and she suffers deeply from her husband's attitude of denial.

Denial is the very opposite of what a woman—what any person—needs to be open to life and to enjoy the peace and tranquility it should offer. Denial is the very opposite of affirmation, whether directed toward one person, toward a group, or toward a social process. Denial is usually an attempt to gain control. Women today do not want to be controlled; they want to be independent in thought and feeling and to be consulted about their own futures. They want to be affirmed and not possessed. They want to be affirmed and not denied.

As a woman and as a psychiatrist, I am aware that society benefits when women are more often affirmed and less often denied, whether as wives, mothers, or wage earners. A denied woman cannot really be the person she is meant to be.

To be truly free, a woman must find affirmation through the love of others and in so doing affirm all of humanity. Here lies the healing for all women and all men. My colleague, Reverend Dr. Thomas A. Kane has written:

> Having been affirmed by another and affirming others, I will know and feel who I am; I will have a true identity. I will sense that I am different but acceptable; that I belong in the world and that I am contributing to it and can change it; that there is a unique place for me and that I have a unique contribution; that I can choose freely to love and to do; that I cannot be ultimately destroyed. I am confidently open to what is to come.[1]

Women are in radical opposition to any movement or person who would deny them as individuals in today's world. I use the term "radical" in the true sense of the meaning of the word, derived from the Latin *radix*, meaning at the very root or the essence. At the essence of all womanhood, and indeed of all personhood, is the need to be recognized for who we are. We want to know and to feel that it is good that we are, so that what we do will be meaningful.

Affirmation is the felt goodness of oneself as an individual and of others whom one affirms and accepts as they are, immaturity and shortcomings notwithstanding, so that their potential may be realized. Women today are affirmers of other women, affirmers of men, and affirmers of all God's creation. When women understand affirmation, they understand their own dignity as persons. The essentials of affirmation are trust, recognition, acceptance, appreciation, approval, and reverence. Because in today's world women assume many roles, they are in a unique position. In many cases, they alone are able to point out the error of judging or condemning people and the benefit of allowing them to grow and to be, to succeed and to fail. Women today have been given the opportunity to teach reverence for persons and respect for each individual. If women themselves are not accorded the same reverence and respect, they must assertively—not aggressively, but assertively—stand firm. They must speak with kindness and minister with charity to those who would deny them, but they must not allow any such process of denial of women to continue.

Women must not allow these forces of denial to touch their individual lives and thus affect their families or their marriages. By combating these forces, women can create conditions that facilitate affirmation. They can help create the time and space needed to be present with people, to form friendships, to be with God, and to be alone. Women by their very nature can show the way to affirmation by helping to remind all the world that happiness will be found when all human beings are appreciated for who they are as individuals and not for what they do. In the truest sense, then, women are the significant others to men, to other women, and to their children.

Women and feminine identity

In years past, a woman's identity was seldom separate from that of her husband if she was married or her father if she was single. Today, however, few women are content to let themselves be defined in terms of such relationships. Instead, they seek to establish their own identities, apart from but not necessarily exclusive of their relationships with men. But to establish one's own identity is not to deny one's anatomy. Women are undeniably female by anatomy, and, as such, they share a certain destiny, a certain procreative function. Others will argue that a woman's destiny has little to do with her anatomy, but I remain unconvinced.

In fact, Erik H. Erickson, one of the most influential writers in the field of psychology and psychiatry today, has said that anatomy, history, and personality combined constitute an individual's destiny. Thus, while certainly not defining a woman solely in terms of her procreative function, Erickson reminds us that a woman is never not a woman and that therefore she must integrate her goals, aspirations, and choices in life with her feminine identity. The freer and more mature a woman becomes, the less she will need to define her freedom in terms of possibilities of existence open to men. The mature woman is liberated; she has no need to compete with men. Her true freedom, her true fulfillment lies in being creative with what she uniquely is and has. A woman's anatomy is her destiny only in that it determines one way a woman finds meaning in her life. What a woman chooses to give her life to and for reflects the basic blueprint of her body.

Of course, women interpret their anatomy, the physiological facts of their existence, in various ways. Some find great truth and meaning in the procreative function of their female sexual bodies, in being a mother. Others either reject outright or choose to ignore their life-giving potential. A few have even stated that they adamantly refuse to be thought of by others or to think of themselves as "baby machines."

One reason why women today may react against being identified with procreation is that in the past the dignity, emotions, and even the human rights of women as persons were sacrificed to their purely functional value of bearing children, particularly sons. For years, the fastidious moralism of Victorian and Puritan social philosophy conspired to reduce sexual intercourse to a duty to which women had to submit in order to provide for the continuity of the human race in the least pleasurable way possible. Even in this century, in Germany during the Second World War, hundreds of women were forced to bear children for political reasons. They were encouraged, often viciously, to conceive one child after another by a father supplied by the government, to assure an increased healthy population of white Aryan men for the future of Germany. No wonder today women vigorously resist being used to gratify the political, social, and sexual needs and goals of men.

Yet, however legitimate grievances such as these may be, women can do equal harm by overreacting and advocating the opposite extremist point of view. Women who deny or repress all that concerns their ability to bear life risk serious psychological problems. A woman's body says that she is female; if the rest of her being does not also say it, she will experience conflict. A woman's body expresses her, whether consciously or unconsciously. It is always telling the world that she is a woman. If her attitudes and manners say something else, a deep split occurs: the woman is torn in two directions. She finds it difficult to discover and establish her own identity, for she is seeking it apart from what she really is; she is endeavoring to construct a self more suited to her intellectual tastes than the self she is already. But self-identity that is not firmly grounded in the reality of anatomy is fantasy, and it hinders rather than helps growth toward maturity.

A woman may be so turned in on herself or so insistent upon "living her own life" that she is unable to acknowledge any calling or responsibility to be for others. Neither a professional career, nor social recognition, nor political independence, for example, is incompatible with a woman's basic affirmation of her anatomy. Moreover, to affirm that a woman's body is made for receiving and nurturing life is not to say that every woman is therefore called to have children. Some may choose to remain celibate; there is much validity and power in such a decision whereby the physical reality is transcended in the name of a different form of life-giving. But whatever choice a woman makes, she cannot deny or repress her own body without causing harm to her whole personality and infecting the other areas of her life with a quality of unreality.

Indeed, women are identified in part by the physiological framework of their female bodies. A woman's anatomy provides an essential structure that shapes a woman's response to herself and to the world in which she lives. As a physician and as a woman, I am acutely aware that the female anatomy is different from that of the male. This difference is complementary: it is necessary to the ultimate unity of the human race. Women who deny their anatomy deny half the human race—themselves and other women—in a manner not unlike that by which men denied women for centuries. Instead, women must affirm their anatomy and speak assertively about their role as bearers and nurturers of life. Women will find increasing happiness and fulfillment not as they deny their feminine identity, but rather as they affirm what makes their role in life unique. Only by acknowledging and celebrating their difference from men can women grow and mature themselves and thus contribute to the healthy growth and maturity of society.

Ecclesial women in contemporary society

All members of modern society live in an age of transition, a period of profound change in which human persons are bound to experience the stress, the anxiety, and the insecurity that are a natural consequence of change. We women who are vowed to religious life within the Church are no exception. Especially since Vatican II, ecclesial women have been continually affected by changes not only in their own Church but in the world in general. All this change has caused many individuals to re-examine the difference between a lay woman and a woman dedicated to God by the vows of religion. Certainly today, when many women religious wear indistinguishable dress and enter almost any profession, including medicine, law, politics, social service, and business, this question of difference is particularly pertinent.

The difference between the lay woman and the ecclesial woman is essentially that of calling. The ecclesial woman in the contemporary Church and her witness in the contemporary society point to the sacred dimension of all reality. The woman religious today does not choose her vocation because it offers extraordinary advantages or special privileges. We women religious are drawn by the gift of grace and somehow set apart by the culture; yet at the same time we are mysteriously and deeply involved in the culture in which we live, in order that we might help to keep alive a sense of the power and the presence of Jesus in the world he redeemed. The truth to which we witness is the truth of the abiding presence of Christ among us; the message we carry is the message of the good news of Jesus. We stand in the world as witnesses and as instruments of One far greater than we. The message we bring is not ours alone. It has been given to us as a sacred trust.

Thus, as her primary vocation, the ecclesial woman today is called to be a living sign of the presence of Christ among humanity, a living reminder that truly God has visited his people. To this life of religious witnessing, to this life of discipleship, the ecclesial woman comes as a female, a feminine human being, a woman with a unique viewpoint of the world and a unique contribution to make to the religious heritage of her culture. As we religious are able to make progress in integrating the natural feminine qualities of our personalities with our religious witness, we shall bring a more genuine feminine and religious presence to our vocation among humanity.

The work of a woman religious to better the lot of humanity is her secondary vocation. Thus she is called to proclaim the presence of Christ nonjudgmentally, more by example and lifestyle than by preaching. In a true sense, we can say that the ecclesial woman is that person called by God to affirm other men and woman and all the goodness of society by her very presence.

History has often overlooked this presence of the woman religious and her work. Even the women's movement, so active in its discovery and documentation of the forgotten achievements of American women, has neglected the many women religious who have accomplished so much not only for their Church but for American society in general. Women religious in the United States have founded and managed hospitals, schools, and social agencies that over the years have become multimillion-dollar nonprofit institutions. Women religious have chaired boards and served as chief executive officers. These institutions and the women religious who directed them have often acted as agents of change in society.

Today ecclesial women who have chosen the life of celibate dedication to Church and society are realizing more and more that in many ways they are freer than the married woman to make the needs of the Kingdom of God a primary concern. Women religious give witness to inspiration, courage, guidance, and a deepened sense of the Sacred in their daily lives.

Endnote
1. Thomas Kane, *The Healing Touch of Affirmation* (Whitinsville, Mass.: Affirmation Books, 1976), p. 26.

III.

Leadership for the Future

Chapter Six

Holistic environments for future Church leaders

*L*eadership in the Church is of utmost importance to us today. In an age when many priests and religious have had their lives shaped by the expectations of others rather than by self-discovery, lack real intimacy in their lives, and have chosen their vocation for reasons of security and status rather than out of interest and ability, it is time to take a hard look at seminary and novitiate formation. I would like to make some observations that would lead to more religious and priests showing initiative and other necessary leadership qualities.

In my experience, many priests and women and men religious are workaholics, unable to say no, and suffering from spiritual boredom. They are physically and intellectually flabby, depressed, discouraged, and burnt out. I believe there is much the seminary and novitiate can do to improve the health of tomorrow's Church leaders on all levels. Then men and women will choose religious vocations for what they will become, not for what they will do.

My approach to health is a holistic one. This holistic concept of health is rooted in a person's biology (physical qualities, nutrition, environment), grows and develops in the mind and heart (intellectual and emotional qualities), and flowers in the individual's spiritual life (lifestyle, values, and prayer life).

First dimension: Physical aspect

With the vision of a holistic environment where all factors contribute to health, let us look at the physical environment of the seminary or novitiate to see what is health-giving and health-promoting. Does the place create a first impression of warmth and invitation? Does it show an appreciation of natural beauty? Some seminaries and novitiates were built in a very institutional design, and it is a challenge to find creative ways to use the buildings so that they are comfortable places for people to assemble, with a home-like atmosphere. Silently they can indicate a reverence for beauty, a healthy attitude toward material things. Cheerful colors, tasteful furnishings, plants, all can be utilized with simplicity to create pleasant surroundings. Pictures and statues should represent good taste in art. A picture can have a religious subject, but be an example of poor art. Not all the pictures should be of religious subjects, for this view is too narrow. Some showing the beauties of nature may lift the heart up to God more quickly than those showing portraits of saints.

The physical plant should facilitate socialization among the seminarians or novices, the faculty, and the staff. It should also encourage a life of prayer, contemplation, reflection, study, and a creative use of leisure. Prayer rooms in addition to the chapel can facilitate different styles of prayer. The television room should not also have facilities for listening to music. These areas should be separate, so those using one medium will not disturb others. In addition, there should be places where small groups can sit and talk quietly without interfering with the pleasure of those choosing other means of relaxation.

Attention to holistic health naturally fosters the physical health of the seminarians or novices. What does the administration do to encourage good nutrition and a balanced diet? Nutritionists emphasize the aliveness of the food and point to the value of fresh and living products. In general, the less food is cooked, the more nutritional value it contains. Providing a wide variety of food and putting more emphasis on fruits, vegetables, seeds, nuts, unrefined grains, and protein in the form of chicken or fish rather than beef will foster better eating habits and help to prevent coronary artery disease. Seeing that the novices' and seminarians' basic food needs are met, and encouraging fruit for between-meal snacks rather than sweets and other "junk foods" will help to develop better physical bodies with the proper weight. Better bodies will lead to better body images for the young people who need to become acquainted with their identities as women and men. It would be good for seminarians and novices to learn how to cook if they do not know already. This skill could be invaluable in maintaining good eating habits once they begin their ministries. Perhaps this instruction could be accomplished in nutrition classes, as part of the curriculum.

What is the attitude in the novitiate or seminary toward smoking and drinking? Research indicates that people who have one alcoholic parent will be genetically predisposed to the disease of alcoholism, and we know that this is a problem for many people today. Exercise should be encouraged, especially sports which can be engaged in alone or with one other person, such as tennis and biking. One of the best aerobic exercises, important for cardiovascular health, is brisk walking or jogging.

Other means of relaxation and the creative use of leisure time should be encouraged. By relaxation I do not mean exercise, but simply quiet, gentle hours. Young people should learn to *be*—to reflect, and use this time to develop talents in art, music, crafts; to appreciate nature—the woods, the ocean, the mountains, whatever is available. Perhaps they would enjoy a hobby—gardening, writing, painting, or some such interest.

Lessons in healthy self-regulation can be taught so that the young people learn to handle distress in a healthy way and take responsibility for their own well-being. They can be shown that it is not their life experiences that influence their good or bad health so much as their own response to those experiences. They can choose to act in a positive or a negative way. We know that in America today cigarettes, alcohol, tranquilizers, and food all help to relieve feelings of distress, but these so-called remedies tend to become problems themselves through their habit-forming properties. More effective is a person's own positive reaction to circumstances.[1]

Second dimension: Intellectual aspect

The second dimension of seminary or novitiate life, the intellectual or academic one, should probably be least criticized. Today's priests and religious, the products of yesterday's seminaries and novitiates, are usually adequately prepared intellectually. If anything, men and women religious are strongest in their intellectual lives, if considered separately from their physical and psychological-spiritual lives. They are often hypertrophied intellectuals but emotional midgets. In fact, these men and women will sometimes use intellectual defenses when dealing with their emotional conflicts.

However, a few points concerning the intellectual or academic life need to be mentioned.

1. A spirit of cooperation is more healthy than a spirit of competition.
2. The relationship of the teacher to student should not be that of the strong to the weak.
3. Learning should be related to living. We need to educate the young, not merely to train them.

Integration of the intellectual with the physical and psychological-spiritual aspects of living is necessary. The young people should not only be educated academically, but helped to integrate the various aspects of their lives into a healthy whole. Besides the traditional curriculum, subjects such as psychology, nutrition, human sexuality, and death and dying should be included. The novices and seminarians need to be convinced that education is an ongoing process. So many parishes today are stagnating because their religious leaders have not stayed abreast of theological and liturgical developments, and have made only superficial concessions to Vatican II.

I hope students will be encouraged to develop an intellectual curiosity and an attitude of openness to new developments both within and outside the Church. It is important to remember that in the seminary or novitiate men and women learn not only factual subjects, but attitudes toward learning and its integration into their daily lives. To motivate a hunger and thirst for learning in depth could be one of the greatest services provided for young people. Besides leading to a degree in some cases, learning can be an encounter with both self and others, in that the student has something to offer to the professor as well as receive.

Third dimension: Spiritual-psychological aspect

The third dimension of novitiate and seminary life, relationships on the spiritual-psychological level, is the broadest to deal with. Faculty members are often role models for students. Students will unconsciously accept the faculty's attitude toward themselves as "standard" for religious life. Women and men religious often know what it means to be a religious, but they lack a separate personal identity.

Because teachers are authority figures, the students may see them as father or mother figures and transfer something of their relationship with their parents onto faculty members. The students' attitudes toward their parents may be hostile, withdrawn, rebellious, or fearful. If the professors are healthy, integrated individuals, there will be healing going on in their daily contacts with the students. A climate for development will be present, so healing takes place in the educative process.

Young people are keen to sense undercurrents in the lives of those around them. They will register anything like apostolic jealousy among the staff members, or antagonism toward authority. A team effort is needed to provide a model for future team ministry, and interdependence among staff members is essential. The staff members need to be sure of their own identity, to appreciate the importance of intimacy, and to be able to deal effectively with both sexes. If a staff member is fearful of women, for example, this fear will be perpetuated in the students, even nonverbally. Seminarians and novices sometimes stereotype members of the opposite sex as threats to their celibacy or to their own ministerial competence. Staff members should bring both male and female friends to the novitiate or seminary for a healthier social life. I do not mean dating; I am referring to healthy friendships. If young women and men experience good interpersonal relationships in the novitiate or seminary, they will be better equipped to continue healthy experiences afterwards. Even those who do not choose to remain in religious life will have received valuable principles and insights that will benefit them, no matter what choices they may make in the future. Faculty members' support systems need to include people from outside the learning environment as well as from within. Otherwise, the system would be an unhealthy one.

It would be good for the staff to have an intercommunication support system. Every two weeks the staff could gather and air feelings of anger or of joy. Emotions sometimes considered negative or uncomfortable would come out here in a healthy way, rather than be indicated in other unhealthy ways. The staff would need to develop a trust level such that they could reveal what is meaningful for them to one another.

Thus each member of the seminary or novitiate staff needs to deal with attitudes toward self and toward other staff members. What does each one do to foster a holistic approach to daily life? What I said earlier about continuing education for the seminarians and novices applies as well to the staff. What is each one doing to stay alive intellectually, emotionally, spiritually? Encouraging research and development by the faculty would be beneficial to everyone. The novitiate or seminary must foster a healthy environment, and each person must take a share of responsibility for the task. Do staff members have strong identities as persons or do they depend on their roles as professors or administrators? Because of the far-reaching effects of their influence on future Church leaders, staff members should be quick to seek counseling if they have personal problems in these areas, or with celibacy or their relationships with men or women.

How staff members relate to students is important. A certain reserve is necessary, but humanness also. It is possible to relate on a social level without compromising one's position. Instead of being aloof, staff members can spend time listening, establishing trusting relationships, and accepting students where they are in their development. Staff members must be mature. They should encourage students to talk informally about topics that are treated in the classroom, to examine honestly their attitudes and feelings.

Today's seminarians and novices will share the virtues and faults of their contemporaries. They are subjective, immature, intolerant, dogmatic, much more docile, and less critical than the students of the sixties. They do not need to stay this way, of course. The novitiate or seminary should be a place where the students can mature, with helpful guidelines for living, and opportunities to take personal responsibility for their decisions. In our candidate assessments at the House of Affirmation, we find many future seminarians and novices to be passive personalities with no firm sexual identities. They need to have counseling available, and the climate should be such that they can talk about human sexuality. Lectures should be offered on topics of concern, such as homosexuality, heterosexuality, masturbation, and celibacy, and time allowed afterwards for discussion.

A career choice is something that is made not once, but over and over again. Notice the number of men and women making career changes in midlife today. Again, when they near retirement age for one career, some choose to enter upon another. Perhaps the opportunities presented for ministry while in the novitiate or seminary could afford the young people choices as to what they will do and how much time they feel they can devote to it. Of course, they should be supervised if they are to move toward personal maturity. Both peers and superiors can supervise a student, and professors and administrators should be willing to have students evaluate their work in the classrooms and offices. The students' areas of weakness should be dealt with gradually as they are met, and not left for a few major confrontations during their formation. Once the seminarian is ordained or the novice professed, some system should be set up for continued supervision. Because the first year is so crucial, the newly-ordained or professed should be carefully placed and should be able to give some input on the best use of their abilities, as they see them. Young people should have a place to discuss problems as they arise, and before they loom too large.

Everyone living in the learning community should be concerned with developing a climate of trust. Friendships should be encouraged, not considered divisive. Sometimes when two novices or seminarians are seen together, a suspicion of homosexuality is raised without grounds. Distrust can be generated by implying things not present.

An important principle of holistic health is that a person can be whole and healthy spiritually, no matter what personality faults or handicaps that individual has. The expression "spiritual well-being" indicates wholeness, and dependence on God in contrast to fragmentation and isolation.

Spiritual well-being is the affirmation of life, saying yes to life, even to adverse circumstances. This attitude is not optimism which denies or overlooks life's realities. Rather, it is the acknowledgment of the destiny of life. In the light of that destiny, spiritual well-being is the love of one's own life, and the lives of others, and concern for one's community, society, and the whole of creation. A person's affirmation of life is rooted in participating in a community of faith. In such a community, one grows to accept the past with its pluses and minuses, to be aware and alive in the present, and to live in hope of fulfillment. Everyone is called to respond to God in love and obedience. How much more should Church leaders love and obey the God who calls them.

Realizing all are God's children, seminarians and novices can grow toward wholeness as individuals as they come to affirm their kinship with others in the community of faith as well as the entire human family. They affirm life in the context of their relationships with God, self, community, and environment. They see God as the creator of life, the source and power who wills well-being. Under God and as members of the community of faith, they are responsible to relate all the resources of the environment to the well-being of humanity. So often women and men religious must struggle with an unattainable ideal image placed before them by others, when they are constantly experiencing their own human frailty. Their learning environment should not offer an ideal of performance and life which they cannot duplicate in their ministries. It is unhealthy to fill young men and women with false expectations about an unrealistic future. The staff should emphasize that human wholeness is never fully attained. All through life this wholeness is a possibility in the process of becoming. The staff should teach the students to see the possibilities in reality—this is the way to find meaning in life.

Spiritual leadership

Because novices and seminarians will become spiritual leaders in the Church, they need good role models in the leaders they encounter in the novitiate or seminary. In such a community, spiritual leadership is the responsibility of all the members. It presupposes that the community as a whole is more concerned about the presence of the spirit, the morale in its midst, than about structure, organization, or efficiency.

There are three aspects to spiritual leadership:
1. Awakening people to their call to what God intended them to be in illness and in wellness, in tragedy and in joy;
2. The ability to challenge;
3. The ministry of healing.

Novices and seminarians need to be encouraged to use all their gifts, talents, and potential talents of body, mind, and soul to respond to the Spirit. As Paul tells us, "All of you, then, are Christ's body and each one is part of it" (I Cor. 12:27). Each one is essential to the integrity of the whole. To awaken people to their call is to help them to become aware of their gifts, and to show them how they can serve the kingdom in weakness as well as in strength. To do this is to affirm them. Affirming others helps them to find meaning in life, to find a possibility in reality. To call another to a healthy life requires a great sensitivity to the individual. It means that we constantly help one another to find the real meaning in our lives, the different calls of the Spirit, which bring about a diversity and pluriformity that enrich. Thus each individual is encouraged to become the unique being for which God gave the potential.

A second function of spiritual leadership is to challenge others, in order to help preserve the kind of life needed to live out the gospel message. In challenging people, we must concentrate on asking questions rather than giving answers. "Do you want to follow Christ?" The reply to that question must be an answer of faith, given as the person takes a leap into the dark of insecurity. When we provide such leadership we disturb others. But we will also help to preserve and enhance the response given to the gospel.

The third function of spiritual leadership is a ministry of healing. Before men and women can work in ministry, they need to be members of a psychotheological healing community so that the healing will overflow into their ministry. There are so many people who feel unaccepted, out of place, emotionally disturbed, mentally ill, lonely, and inadequate, that the ministry of healing becomes one of the most important functions of leadership. Seminarians and novices are often not so far in age from high school and college students, and we know that depression among young people, even to the point of an increase in their suicides, is a national problem today. Leadership can no longer express itself in authoritarian terms; it must make the compassion and the forgiveness of God visible and credible.

Preparation for the future

One of the intangible tasks of the novitiate or seminary is to prepare men and women for the future. They need to find meaning, and they will not find it in the old tasks of religious life. More and more in this complex world women and men religious find they must specialize, and there is even more danger of their becoming immersed in tasks not directly related to their chosen ministry. Counseling for the career choices open to them is important, but it is not enough. The attitudes inculcated in the seminary or novitiate will be the ones the young people bring to their ministries, attitudes that will most affect their lives. For that reason, the novitiate or seminary should model a leisurely, appreciative attitude toward life, not merely one of efficiency.

Another aspect of the future will be the young priest's, brother's, or sister's living situation. No matter how health-giving and wholesome the seminary or novitiate environment is, the young person must face the fact that in the future, living with many of his or her fellow religious or priests will be difficult, if not nearly impossible. Some pastors and superiors are still living in pre-Vatican II days; others are true workaholics immersed in tasks, or struggling with alcoholism, lonely and unhappy. With the help of their formation, young people can find other possibilities for friendship, and continue the wholesome habits of a balanced diet, good nutrition, sufficient exercise, and intellectual and spiritual pursuits. If students are given the opportunity for ministry experience during their training, they will obtain a more realistic picture of what their living possibilities will be. Above all, they will need to be open to growing in the future, and allowing others to grow as well.

On the other side of the picture, religious leaders need to work out good relationships with the newly-ordained or professed. Concern for the young people will be evident in their placement, continued supervision, and encouragement to educate themselves, perhaps by inviting them back to the seminary or novitiate for programs which will help to motivate them to keep abreast of new ideas. The possibilities of team ministry should be explored.

Is some type of "ideal" priest or religious presented to the seminarians or novices as a model? It is so important to prevent this stereotyping, to which some young people are already inclined. Involving the students in decision-making, such as setting up living guidelines, is another way to prepare them for the future. It is a psychological truism that one who shares in a decision will be more motivated to carry it out. Even if everyone does not agree with the final decision, the opportunity to air feelings will help clear the air, and persons, satisfied that they were listened to, will cooperate with the choice made.

Dr. Paul Tournier has said that "spirituality means looking for relationships and recognizing that it is our relationship to God which gives meaning to nature." He goes on to observe, "What is spiritual in us is our need for relationships—with our neighbour, with nature, with society, and with God. This, I think, is the broadest definition of spiritual life. It is what makes us a real person. . . ."[2]

I stress relationships because religious professionals come into contact with so much tragedy in their ministry. They are confided in, turned to, leaned upon, and looked to for strength and encouragement in times of suffering and death. Such a burden is too much for any one person without a strong certainty of the meaning of life and a close relationship with God. Only if one has this sense of purpose, of confidence in the goodness of God despite all appearances, can one affirm others in their time of sorrow for any length of time.

Healers

Today the medical profession is becoming more aware that it is the whole person, body, mind, and soul, who must be healed. Also, we are beginning to realize that sometimes health professionals may be less effective than another person who listens, shows concern, and is completely present to the one in need. Henri Nouwen has said that "we all are healers who can reach out to offer health, and we all are patients in constant need of help. Only this realization can keep professionals from becoming distant technicians and those in need of care from feeling used or manipulated."[3] Religious or priests will surely be such a healing presence in ministry if they have been shown this attitude in the novitiate or seminary.

Members of the learning community may complain of loneliness, an impersonal atmosphere, or a lack of community, and express a desire for support, and someone with whom to share experiences. In such instances they may well be hiding their own healing talents through fear or a lack of confidence. They need to deal with these problems because loneliness is also one of the greatest problems of religious life. Here the most important thing we can do for others is to show interest in their joys and pains, pleasures and sorrows, all that has given shape and form to their lives and brought them to their present situations. As Nouwen observes, "This is far from easy because not only our own but also other people's pains are hard to face." We would prefer "to offer advice, counsel, and treatment to others without having really known fully the wounds that need healing."[4]

Listening is an art that must be developed. It needs the real presence of people to one another. Young men and women in religious formation should be encouraged to show compassion, openness, real interest, and a willingness to listen and speak to each other. In this way they will affirm one another, accepting each other as they are, without false expectations.

If the novitiate or seminary is a place where all are affirmed, then these health-giving relationships will help religious and priests develop a holistic approach to life, one that will enable them to become well-rounded leaders in the Church, with a wholesome influence wherever they may serve.

Endnotes

1. See Hans Selye, M.D., "Self-Regulation: The Response to Stress," in *Inner Balance: The Power of Holistic Healing,* Elliott M. Goldwag, ed. (Englewood Cliffs, N.J.: Prentice-Hall, 1979).

2. Dr. Paul Tournier, "Relationships: The Third Dimension of Medicine," *Contact* 47 (October 1978):2.

3. Henri J. M. Nouwen, *Reaching Out* (Garden City, N.Y.: Doubleday, 1975), p. 65.

4. Ibid., p. 67.

Holistic health is an individual commitment. All persons must take the responsibility to make changes in their lifestyle and environment to bring about health. Self is the source for cure. The physician and psychotherapist are really teachers who bring patients to the realization of their own strength and wholeness.

ENVIRONMENT
Housing—Food
Individual
Community

HEALTH AND ILLNESS
Physical   (
Mental   (Preventive
Spiritual   (Curative
    physician/surgeon
    psychiatrist/psychologist
    spiritual director
    pastoral minister
    religious educator

SATISFACTORY MINISTRY
Individual goals   (Interest
Community goals   (Aptitude
Parish goals   (Physical
Diocesan goals   (Mental
    Diversity   (Psychological
    Pluraformity   (Spiritual

LEISURE—CELEBRATION
Vacations
Retreats/Reflection days
Physical exercise
Liturgical experiences
Music/Art/Dance
Hobbies

COMMUNICATIONS
Individual responsibility
Leadership responsibility
    friendship—intimacy
    woman to woman
    man to man
    man and woman

    affirmation—joy
        anger
        sadness/compassion
        listening/hope

Health is a value word; it involves choices because resources are limited. It concerns the quality of life together, with other religious communities, parishes, neighborhoods, laity, both nationally and internationally. We need one another, one another's service. The virtues of faith, hope, and love are involved in health.

EDUCATION—FORMATION

Preparatory	(New Candidates
Continuing	(Professed
Theoretical	(Ordained
Experiential	(Family members
Professional	(Parishioners
Spiritual	(Those in midlife transition
	(career change
	(pre-retirement
	(retirement

PRAYER LIFE	*GOVERNMENT—PARTICIPATORY*
Individual	Constitutions
Community	Vows
Rectory	Diocesan policies for clergy
Parish	Diocesan policies for laity
Family	Family regulations

STEWARDSHIP
FINANCIAL RESPONSIBILITY

Personal	(
Community	(
Parish	(accountability
Family	(

CARE IN RETIREMENT
Terminal illness . . . Dying . . . Death

Chapter Seven

Psychotheological community

$\mathcal{T}$he Second Vatican Council evinced a deep awareness of the solidarity and unity of humankind. In the first article of its basic document, the *Dogmatic Constitution on the Church (Lumen Gentium)*, the Church is presented as "a sign of intimate union with God and of the unity of all mankind [sic]. She is also an instrument for the achievement of such union and unity" (LG, Art I). The thought is further elaborated in its article pertaining to the priesthood of the people of God (LG, Art 10), and that of the priestly community (LG, Art 11). Solidarity also underlies the discussion of collegiality which rests not so much on the legal-juridical notion of a body of coequal colleagues as on the theological development of the doctrine of the Mystical Body where the head and members have different positions and functions but work together in harmony (LG, Art 22).

The *Pastoral Constitution on the Church in the Modern World (Gaudium Spes)* captures the solidarity theme in its opening statement: "The joys and the hopes, the griefs and the anxieties of the men [sic] of this age" are ours (GS, Art 1). The Council reminds us that human dignity comes from our "call to communion with God" (GS, Art 19). The interdependence of all people is explained in terms of interpersonal communion (GS, Art 23) and the communitarian nature of vocation (GS, Art 24).

However, the Council members were aware of the changed and changing conditions of our historical period; reference is made to technology which is transforming the face of the earth, to the advances in biology, psychology, and the social sciences for improving self-knowledge and the life of social groups (GS, Art 5). "Recent psychological research explains human activity more profoundly" (GS, Art 54).

A similar social-psychological concern permeates the *Decree on the Appropriate Renewal of the Religious Life (Perfectae Caritatis)*. "The manner of living, praying, and working should be suitably adapted to the physical and psychological conditions of today's religious . . . to the needs of the apostolate, the requirements of a given culture" (PC, Art 3). With regard to chastity, the decree states: "The religious should take advantage of those natural helps which favor mental and bodily health. . . . Everyone should remember that chastity has stronger safeguards in a community when true fraternal love thrives among its members" (PC, Art 12). It is evident that the seed of a psychotheological community was planted in the conciliar decrees.

The expression "psychotheological community" implies a common quest for communion with God and with others. It informs the religious professional of the fact that personhood can only be realized in community where unity is respectful of the diverse gifts of its members. The establishment of interpersonal relationships constitutes the first step in building community. While being present to and sharing with one another, all members contribute to the community while each person remains a unique individual; it is the unitive bond of common religious values and the friendliness of the community members that brings out and enriches what is unique in each individual.

Agreed, a religious community cannot form the person although it should provide a setting in which the individual human being can emerge as a fully functioning adult. For too long religious communities have lived in a task-oriented rather than a person-oriented environment. Yet, personal development is a basic prerequisite to a meaningful life in the community where the celibate lives. This follows logically from the principle that love of self precedes love of others. But we can only know ourselves if another reveals us to ourselves just as we can only come to a real love of ourselves when we realize that we are loved by another. In the same way we find meaning and a sense of identity in and through others. A person-oriented group helps us appreciate our personhood through the truth and goodness of others who release our powers of knowing and loving. Interpersonal relationships are of utmost importance for personal growth and integration.

While modern life intensifies and augments the deleterious process of depersonalization and dehumanization, no other age has proved more aware of the uniqueness and importance of the individual person. In our age of personalism, we strongly desire to be accepted as a person and not as an object to be exploited. In the past, such personal consciousness took the form of individualism which is the very opposite of Christian charity. The basic premise of individualism rests on the centering of the individual on him or herself so as to guarantee isolation and unlimited freedom. Personalism, on the other hand, insists upon our extending ourselves to others. As Martin Buber would have it, "all real living is meeting." The *I* meets the *thou* of the other and the encounter gives rise to the *we* of community. It is precisely in this union of two spirits that we discover our own spiritual resources. We exist only insofar as we exist for others.

A psychotheological community should model its interpersonal relationships on the loving dialogue within the Trinity where the three persons are one: the Father expresses his thought in the person of the Son and their bond of love is the Holy Spirit. There is no question of seniority or juridical structure; the triune life of God consists precisely in the contemplation of the *thou.* The Father is fully himself while imparting all his power, wisdom, and love to his Son. The Son is entirely himself by receiving his being from the Father and giving himself back to him in love; the Holy Spirit is that bond of love.

So we as religious professionals and as Christian personalists, find our true selves by looking to Christ who is loved by the one who personifies love. Christian personalism is characterized by the I-we-thou relationship; in the presence of God, we affirm that all we are and have is an expression of God's love. That is why we must regard the personal gifts with which we have been endowed as bestowed in view of the Mystical Body; our gifts and charisms were given and intended for service to our own community and to the Church.

God wants to bring each one of us to the fulfillment of our calling through a message of love which involves others. We are therefore unable to find our *thou* in God, who alone can make us happy, if we do not contact God's beloved messenger, our colleague. We cannot fully actualize ourselves by exploiting our neighbors, by using them as stepping stones to our personal enhancement. If we open ourselves to others and to their dignity, we come to a genuine restoring experience of ourselves.

The concept of collegiality bears significance for life in a psychotheological community. All of us have the right to explain our wishes if, by our good ideas, we can contribute to the good of the parish or the local community. Every member of the community should be encouraged to bear his or her share of responsibility, to contribute within the realm of his or her competence to the welfare of the group. Collegiality is an expression of love and it implies a relationship of trust. There is a mutual solidarity when all assume responsibility for the common good. The relationship of religious leaders to other community members within the community must therefore be one of true love. Each one must be accepted with good qualities and imperfections. We should never look to the faults of another without first seeking a deeper awareness of our own imperfections and mistakes. It is the basis for a truthful acceptance of one another as we are; only then can we give mutual help to become more fully what Christ wants us to be.

Openness in interpersonal relationships necessitates finding time to listen to people; for this to be done correctly, we must listen to the Holy Spirit and meditate on the Gospel. Superiors or pastors have no monopoly on insights; they will learn docility to the Spirit by being docile to fellow religious and colleagues.

With humility, a superior or pastor can listen to others especially when they are eager and able to contribute.

Religious professionals are called to witness to the essential nature of the Church. Psychotheological communities must demonstrate maturity, proving that they are made up of responsible persons in the discipleship of Christ where there exists great respect for the human person. Growth toward maturity means moving toward a commitment that involves the whole of ourselves, a commitment to the truth of our life, to God. As religious professionals, then, we must find ourselves. We must establish our identity. Each of us embodies a thought in the mind of God and all our life will be a struggle to measure up to divine expectations. Ultimately, the life of a religious professional represents a unique extension of Christ's life manifested to the world.

In the search for maturity, we move from a selfish to an altruistic mode of action. We shift our emotional center from an intense preoccupation with self-value to attention to the value-of-the-other. It is a movement from undue concern for the self to that of the community. In the depth of our relationship with another, both of us experience a gradual deepening and opening of personality.

Eriksonian psychology maintains that in order to experience close interpersonal relationships, we must have a reasonable sense of personal identity. Those of us who have failed to develop an identity will avoid close interpersonal relations; the surer we are of ourselves, the more we will seek interpersonal relationships where we can express ourselves with spontaneity and warmth because we are capable of a real and mutual exchange of love. My clinical experience has proved to me that most priests and religious are wanting in this aspect of personal development. I have also witnessed what the psychotheological therapeutic community of the House of Affirmation has contributed to the emotional growth and maturity of residents.

The friendships of a religious professional are of a special type in that they are ultimately based upon spiritual values. Consequently, close interpersonal relations among men and women religious presuppose a certain spiritual maturity which, in turn, demands optimal emotional maturity. The latter denotes attainment of a certain healthy balance between extreme emotional states; it suggests the possession of definite qualities which enable persons to preserve peace within themselves and with others. These qualities include decisive thinking, unselfishness, a sense of personal responsibility for the community, temperate emotional reactions, ability to profit from criticism, ability to face reality, and a well-balanced attitude toward both sexes without genital involvement. The possession of these qualities points to our capacity to enter into friendships which will deepen our personal sense of identity and our sense of intimacy; it will also serve to increase self-knowledge.

Since a sense of intimacy results from healthy and mature friendships, it would seem imperative for us to foster and enjoy such friendships if we are to grow in psychological and eventually spiritual maturity. Of course, not all friendships develop a sense of intimacy. Friendship, however, should not be confused with fellowship where the interaction rests on reciprocal interests or mutual advantage; the primary motive, in this case, is selfish.

There is also a type of interpersonal relationship that serves a lubricative function in a group; it keeps the religious machinery going without unnecessary and unfortunate friction. A friendship demonstrating a mature sense of intimacy is characterized by fidelity, trust, and mutual acceptance. There is a consistent forbearance, an ability on the part of the two persons to overlook transitory moods and passing emotional states; there is trust since both parties are willing to allow the other person to see and know their weaknesses and failings, hopes and aspirations. A sense of equality prevents a one-way admiration from developing. In spite of respective gifts of nature and grace, true friends are mutually accepting.

Vatican II has invited all of us to avail ourselves of the insights of the social sciences, specifically psychology, in view of better serving the Church of today. Religious professionals can build a psychotheological community because they share a common value system. Should we be living alone, we owe it to ourselves to seek our fellow religious professionals in the area so as to build community and enjoy the values of true friendship. The solidarity of Church members will gain through friendly exchanges and reciprocated services. Our religious commitment will also be safeguarded by the strong bonds of Christian love.

A living example

The House of Affirmation was founded as a direct outgrowth, broadened in scope, of the Consulting Center for Clergy and Religious of the Diocese of Worcester. The center had been established as the result of a request by the Senate of Religious to Most Rev. Timothy J. Harrington, auxiliary bishop and vicar for religious and Bishop Bernard Flanagan (the Ordinary of the diocese). The religious and clergy of the diocese needed a nonresidential center where they could discuss their emotional, spiritual, and vocational problems with professionals in the behavioral sciences who would understand and appreciate their celibate lifestyle.

The early nonresidential center's overriding goal was to help priests and men and women religious—religious professionals—to become fully human, consistently free persons within the context of their ecclesial calling and of society.

In 1973, the first residential center opened in Whitinsville, Massachusetts. Since then over 1,000 priests, brothers, and sisters have participated in the residential program; about 5,000 nonresidents have come for counseling. Clients sometimes refer themselves to the House of Affirmation (many understand their own problems after reading our books) or are referred by major superiors, bishops, and professionals such as psychiatrists and psychologists.

A unique feature of the House of Affirmation is its psychotheological approach. The residential centers base their programs on the psychotheological therapeutic community. This total community concept goes beyond milieu therapy with its inherent analytic orientation. The whole person lives in a wholly residential therapeutic environment where a similar value system is shared. The expression "psychotheological community" implies a common quest for communion with God and with humans. This psychotheological approach is based on the anthropology of St. Thomas Aquinas, in unity with the magisterium and tradition of the Roman Catholic Church, and in dialogue with the new insights of theology and the best of modern clinical psychiatry and psychology.

Because many priests, brothers, and sisters do not know how to relate socially or intimately, we chose to make the community a mixed group to facilitate the therapeutic process.

Our purpose was to accept individuals where they were, regardless of their liabilities, to accept them for their goodness and for what they could become. The whole environment was to convince these individuals that they could work out their problems. Some priests and sisters had received psychiatric or psychological help elsewhere, even as inpatients, but they were never really healed. The institutions had not addressed the spiritual aspect of their lives, their beliefs, and values. We felt we needed a psychotheological community, and we decided on a holistic approach.

First, the residents' physical needs are met. They have pleasant furniture—nothing luxurious or excessive, but comfortable, homelike, and colorful. The food is wholesome, well-balanced, nourishing, and presented in an appetizing way. As they go into therapy these people suffer a great deal psychologically; they need to have some amenities.

We do not take care of residents' medical problems, but we do have a good medical referral system. At each center the psychiatrist sees every resident and reviews the medical history. It would be terrible to treat someone with psychotherapy and miss a medical diagnosis.

The psychological treatment consists of individual therapy and different types of group therapy, including small group meetings. In weekly community meetings staff members and residents discuss everyday living problems. The center is the residents' home, and they may bring up suggestions or complaints. We work with realities, and we do what has to be done. When we do not do what residents request, they learn how to deal with authority. They also have their own meetings without a staff person present so that they can learn to explore issues at peer level.

We also offer yoga, physical therapy, exercise, psycho-drama, and movement therapy. The purpose of these therapies is to expand the residents' use of their bodies and, in so doing, to expand their feelings. Discovered feelings and the ability to move with other people make residents feel better about them-selves. Some priests, brothers, and sisters are very stiff and afraid to touch others; it is legitimate for them to learn how to relax physically so that their bodies can become spontaneous.

In a weekly spirituality seminar, residents talk about scrip-ture, spiritual life, and prayer and how to integrate them in everyday living. We prefer that residents attend the seminar and the daily liturgy, but they are free not to. In the past, attendance was mandatory in communities; if someone was not at Mass or prayers, people wondered. Religious never really internalized that they go to liturgy because they choose to. They must have that freedom of choice so they can grow. Once every two months they also have a day of recollection.

The House of Affirmation offers much freedom for growth, and sometimes the residents do not know how free they are. When they do realize, they do not know how to use their free-dom. They do not know how to use leisure, nor how to slow down. We encourage pursuing cultural interests, seeing good movies and plays, visiting museums, and taking nature walks.

In the process of group therapy, the residents grow very close. For some, the stay at the House of Affirmation is their first experience of community: they may have been in religious life for twenty years and never experienced the real love, intimacy, and trust that occur in our centers.

We take men and women with emotional, vocational, and spiritual problems. We usually do not take people with a psy-chosis, although we have taken residents who are manic-depressive providing they have been or can be medically stabilized.

We have a three-day psychotheological assessment program at each center. The prospective client comes to the center for a few days, takes a battery of psychological tests, and has interviews with two or three staff members, one of whom is a priest- or sister-psychologist. The assessment committee then meets to decide the diagnosis and recommendations.

We suggest that no one stay for fewer than four months or longer than one year. Most residents stay an average of six to eight months. Although some people have stayed two months, we have found that it takes at least three months for a person to settle down and to adapt to the environment.

While an individual is still in residency, a comprehensive aftercare program is begun. First, diocesan or provincial authorities meet with the resident, the client's individual therapist, and a House of Affirmation aftercare worker to plan for the resident's transition back to the diocese or religious community.

Then, shortly after an individual's departure from the House of Affirmation, an aftercare worker travels to the client's home community or diocese to conduct an aftercare workshop. To insure a smooth transition throughout the initial months after termination, regular phone contact is maintained between House of Affirmation personnel and the client. Annual aftercare workshops aid returning residents to learn necessary skills, and to explore the issues facing them during their reintegration into ministry and community or rectory living.

In aftercare we work to develop appropriate and realistic plans for ministry living situations, and any necessary follow-up treatment. Some former residents continue to see a counselor in their home area periodically. We maintain an updated list of therapists in North America who have an understanding of our ministry and psychotheological approach. Other residents returning to active ministry do not need continued counseling. Still others reside in an area that is near enough to one of our centers for them to continue in outclient therapy with a staff member of the House of Affirmation.

Aftercare also includes opportunities for involvement in a local support group that provides additional mutual support, understanding, and companionship. Many former residents return after several months to one of our centers for a few days to discuss the experience of transition from the House of Affirmation to their new ministry and living situation. Annual Affirmation Weekends provide former residents the opportunity to attend the House of Affirmation symposium and renew old acquaintances and friendships.

People ask me if I see the continued need for the House of Affirmation program. It is true that some seminary and formation directors in religious communities are trying to develop more humane programs, to deal with psychological needs, and to provide an environment where the candidates and new members can grow. But not all congregations and seminaries are yet doing that, and they have not yet developed a balance.

I hope that in the next fifteen to twenty years seminaries and novitiates will have developed a holistic life, meeting physical, psychological, and spiritual needs. I also hope that the people in authority as role models will be mature and integrated themselves. That has been the problem in the past: intellectual giants on the faculty were emotional midgets.

Attention must be paid to providing teachers and mentors who are well-integrated and healthy. Religious leaders cannot be task-oriented any more. They must be person-oriented. The challenge is to integrate behavioral science with sound theology, sound spirituality.

These improved programs may mean not so many people will come to the House of Affirmation in future years. Our educational programs and publications will continue also to do preventative work for clergy and religious as well as laypeople. But there will always be a need for the House because clergy and religious, being human, will experience emotional problems, particularly during transition periods.

Affirmation Books is an important part of the ministry of the House of Affirmation, International Therapeutic Center for Clergy and Religious, founded by Sr. Anna Polcino, M.D., F.A.P.A., and Fr. Thomas A. Kane, Ph.D., D.P.S. Income from the sale of Affirmation books and tapes is used to provide care for priests and religious suffering from emotional unrest.

The House of Affirmation provides a threefold program of service, education, and research. Among its services are five residential therapeutic communities and three counseling centers in the United States and one residential center in England. All centers provide nonresidential counseling.

The House of Affirmation Center for Education offers a variety of programs in ongoing Christian formation. It sponsors a leadership conference each year during the first week of February and a month-long Institute of Applied Psychotheology during July. More than forty clinical staff members conduct workshops and symposiums throughout the year.

For further information, write or call the administrative offices in Natick, Massachusetts:

> The House of Affirmation
> 109 Woodland Street
> Natick, Massachusetts 01760
> 617/651-3893